Doyles

seafood cookbook

recipes & memories from Australia's first family of seafood, **by Alice Doyle**

Doyles

seafood cookbook

HarperCollins*Publishers*

HarperCollins*Publishers*
First published as *Doyle's Fish Cookbook*
by Angus & Robertson Publishers Australia in 1979
Second edition published in 1983
Third edition published in 1989
Fourth (paperback) edition published in 1996
Cornstalk edition published in 1997
Revised in 1999 and 2005

This revised edition published in 2005
by HarperCollins*Publishers* Pty Limited
ABN 36 009 913 517
A member of the HarperCollins*Publishers* (Australia) Pty Limited Group
www.harpercollins.com.au

HarperCollins*Publishers*
25 Ryde Road, Pymble, Sydney, NSW 2073, Australia
31 View Road, Glenfield, Auckland 10, New Zealand
77-85 Fulham Palace Road, London, W6 8JB, United Kingdom
2 Bloor Street East, 20th floor, Toronto, Ontario M4W 1A8, Canada
10 East 53rd Street, New York NY 10022, USA

National Library of Australia Cataloguing-in-Publication data:

Doyle, Alice.
   Doyles seafood cookbook
   Rev. ed.
   Includes index.
   ISBN 0 7322 7120 7.
   1. Cookery (Seafood). 2. Cookery (Fish). I. Title.
641.692

Book design by de Luxe & Associates
Front cover photograph copyright © Matt King; seafood images on spine and back cover copyright © Karl Schwerdtfeger;
front flap photograph by Christine Orchard; back flap photograph courtesy of the Doyle family
Photographs on pages 6, 26, 28, 38, 58, 105 and 142 © Karl Schwerdtfeger
Photographs on pages 9, 35, 45, 65, 73, 90, 99, 130, 135 and 154 copyright © Marco Bok
Photographs on pages 10, 16, 17, 19 and 22 courtesy of the Doyle family
Photographs on pages 13 and 14 courtesy of the Woollahra Library Local History Collection
Matt King, Marco Bok and Karl Schwerdtfeger have asserted their moral rights to be identified as the authors of their
respective photographs

Printed in China by Phoenix Offset on 128gsm Chinese Matt

5 4 3 2 1 05 06 07 08

Dedication

*T*o my dear sister Flo and to everyone connected with the seafood business.

I know exactly what it's like to be 'the lady from the fish shop'. So here's to the fish folk — all those people who depend on fish for a living. I know just how you all feel at times. We live with it, handle it, catch it, clean it, sell it, explain the species, and answer the constant question, 'Is it fresh?' (As if we would say 'No'!) It's worse when you have a restaurant. With all the sea around you, the customers can't understand why John Dory is not on today, or there are no lobsters. 'But why?' they ask, after I explain about seasonal shortages and huge seas. 'The Harbour seems so calm.'

Congratulations especially to the fish cleaners, who do such a good job in preparing the fish for people to cook. You try to live down that unmistakable smell of fish when you meet your mates at the local for a schooner or two after a day's hard work, and then you head home for a hot shower and a clean up, knowing you have to leave those smelly old gumboots outside the back door and your clothes in the laundry. You don't dare go in the house first — Mum and the family will see to that.

I know all about that smell — how many times do we all wish we were in the chemist's line of business, and smelling like it. But, folks, we're stuck with it! And after all, nowadays seafood is luxury food, and a couple of decent crayfish with a mud crab thrown in are more expensive than a small-sized bottle of Joy — for many years, the world's most expensive perfume.

Contents

The Harvest from the Sea

Australia is noted all over the world for its fabulous foods from the sea. When I think of the oceans surrounding our continent, and especially when I sail on our beautiful Pacific, I think of all that lives under that azure blue water. No wonder you don't have to cook your fish for long – they don't develop any tough muscles; for them swimming is easy work. And, you know, fish aren't so dumb; they eat very well (so if I were you I'd bathe between the flags). The sea is rich in vitamins, minerals and proteins, and fish collect all these valuable nutrients when they eat. When we eat them, we benefit from their collection.

The delicate flavour of fish and shellfish, plus their low-kilojoule, high-energy content, make dieting with seafood a natural. Just one serving provides nearly all the protein needed each day to help build and repair body tissue. In addition to being rich in vitamins and minerals, seafoods are low in fats and high in 'fill-ability'.

Weather and seasons play a big part in our supply of seafoods. At times your favourite species of fish or shellfish becomes scarce and expensive, though often no more expensive than the better cuts of meat. There are also seasons when some kinds of fish become plentiful – fish like mullet and gemfish, for example, at which some people – 'fish snobs' – turn up their noses. But don't be put off these fish, because so many delicious dishes can be made using them. Have a look at some of my recipes in this book.

New Australians from all over the world have introduced us old Australians to lots of seafoods that once we would not have thought of eating. Once I could not walk on the rocks bounding the sea around our area because the oysters, sea eggs, pippies and other shellfish would cut my feet to pieces when I went barefoot (what other way?). And those ockies (octopus) I would find in crevices and old tins – I'd just lift them up on a stick and throw them back into the water. There were always dozens of squid hanging around your fishing line, and you couldn't stand catching them because of all that black ink you were certain to be squirted with. Now all these creatures are considered delicacies – and priced like them – and those same rocks are practically smooth. It makes you think. Times change, but fish is now, more than ever, Australia's national food.

I hope this book will help 'sell' seafoods – and good health – to you all.

Early one foggy winter morning, Pyrmont Fish Market

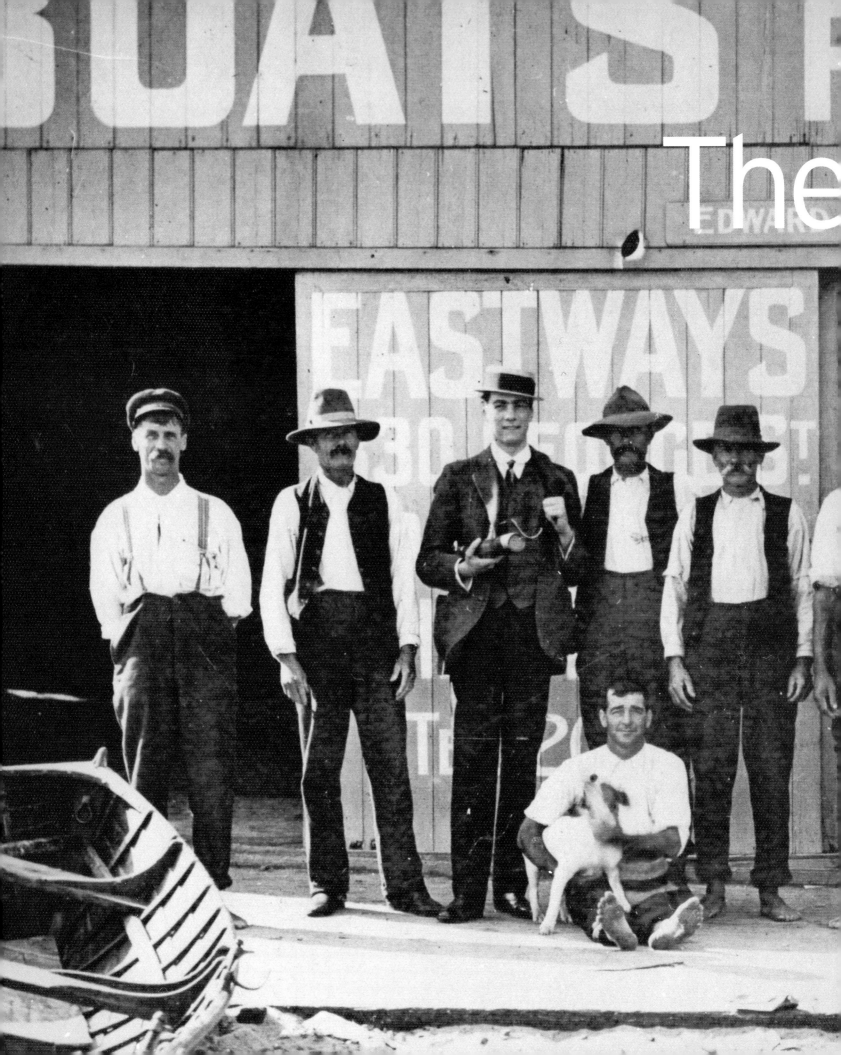

Story of Doyles

My grandparents opened their first cafe in the same spot Doyles stands now.

*W*hen, in the early 1970s, I told my husband and my family that I was writing this book, they said, 'Well, go ahead, Mum – if you don't know about seafood by now after all these years, you may as well give up the game!'

I was fortunate enough to have been born in Watsons Bay, Sydney, at a time when lots of professional fishermen lived there. I was brought up with my three sisters and two brothers at that old-fashioned cafe that still sits on Marine Parade, Watsons Bay, with a tin overhanging roof supported by posts. It used to be called the Ozone Cafe – now it's Doyles on the Beach. It's not an imposing building by any means. No architect ever drew plans for it. Wilky Schweers, a well-known carpenter and a much loved and respected citizen of the Bay (and, of course, married to one of Mum's relations), worked on it.

We all love the place, and I hope it will stay and be repaired and renewed over the years and that no council or planning scheme will make my family remove it. When the westerly gales are on and the storms whip up a huge sea, I always say a prayer for the little cafe – and so far so good, because it keeps on being there, intact, when everything's calm again.

It was a few years ago that we changed its name to Doyles on the Beach, to distinguish it from our restaurant on the wharf at Watsons Bay. So many Sydney people from all walks of life visit this beautiful spot, and, of course, many overseas and interstate visitors come to sit on the beachfront to enjoy their lunch, too. The setting is unique, and I am sure it equals in beauty and charm any other waterside eating spot in

the world. Gazing up the Harbour to the city of Sydney, watching the huge container ships coming and going and the ferries and small pleasure craft moving around, is fascinating and relaxing.

No wonder our customers often don't want to leave and sit lingering over a cup of coffee until sunset. I think the old restaurant on the beach has such an atmosphere – at times I'm sure it's haunted by my late grandparents and parents. They loved it so, like we all do.

Grandfather and Grandmother Newton opened their first little cafe in a tiny shop on that same spot on the Watsons Bay promenade in the late 1880s. Ferries, notably the *Bee* and the *Fairy Queen*, used to bring picnic parties to the Bay, so Grandma did a little business at the shop in the fine weather, and Grandfather fished. They had a fuel stove out the back, and they used to cook scones and fry fish and chips for the picnickers. Most of the fuel they used came from the beachfront – driftwood and coke.

My grandfather's love of the sea was strong in him, as it is in me.

Grandfather Newton had a hut on land belonging to the Wentworth Estate in Coolong Road, Vaucluse. He mended his nets there. Grandfather used to take the VIPs of Sydney out fishing, and then he would bring them back to the hut and would make his famous soup with the bones and heads and scraps from some of the fish he'd caught. He'd fry the fillets and serve them with the soup. I still have Grandfather's recipe for that soup, as my mother made it for many years at the restaurant (bouillabaisse recipe page 43). I often wonder how much he charged for those lovely day's outings and that delicious meal he put on afterwards. Of course, I don't know what they drank – no fancy wines, I suppose, like today – but I'm sure Grandfather Newton after a hard (call it hard) day's fishing and sailing with his party would have always made sure there was a hot toddy to warm everybody up and start the old fish yarns off.

They reckon my grandfather bent his elbow too much and didn't see all that cheap land known as the Vaucluse Estate being sold all around him, with prices starting at thirty shillings an acre. I don't care about that – what

Previous pages: The Watsons Bay boatshed, 1900

does it matter? He was a good grandfather and was much loved. He enjoyed his life, and the love of the sea was strong in him, like it is in me. I drive everybody crazy at times admiring sunrise and sunset and the moon on the Harbour, and feeding the seagulls. (Seagulls down our way are choosy nowadays – they won't have bread, but hold out for fish pieces left over from the restaurants. I get into trouble for feeding them because it encourages them onto the boats – I must admit they do make a mess.)

The Smith brothers came and settled in Watsons Bay, and they, along with Grandfather, net-fished all the inlets of the Harbour. Of course, there were lots of pilots and fishermen living in Watsons Bay, on the water's edge, at that time. By pilots I mean the pilots that used to take the sailing ships up to the port of Sydney. They all tendered for the jobs and, in between waiting for ships to come in, lots of them fished and stayed at Camp Cove beach.

The Smith brothers were hard-working and they looked the part – suntanned and healthy to look at. (When I was a kid, they always reminded me of the label on that well-known cod liver oil mixture. As I write this, I can even taste it! It must have been cheap to buy – everybody had a bottle in the house.) You would see the Smith brothers and some of their crew out practically every day. They worked hard, and seemed to be out in all weathers, even with an easterly gale. Those easterly gales used to cause a big drawback of the water on the beach down in Watsons Bay, and I found them frightening.

There was always lots of anticipation as the nets were pulled in, and the sight always attracted a crowd. You would see two hefty men standing on the beach yards apart, pulling the net gently, and a couple of the crew on the rowing boats standing up, oars working slowly, as the net was hauled in. Sometimes there was a good catch: bream, whiting, silver bream, black bream, sand flathead and always plenty of seaweed. (Really we should eat seaweed, but I can't give you a recipe – I've never sort of fancied it.) In the nets, as well as the fish, there would be lots of exciting odds and ends, such as seahorses, sea stars, squid and octopus. There used to be an Italian man down there who would go and buy squid and octopus from the Smiths. I used to screw up my nose at that, in those days, but I have learned differently now . . .

After the haul, the net fishermen had to take up their nets and put them on the rails of the Watsons Bay wharf

1880s

Above: My grandparents' tearooms in the 1880s

to dry. Then they'd clean them and pick out all the debris they'd collected in the sea. (Now, before you rush out to buy a net, you'd better ring the fish marketing authority in your State/Territory and find out about the rules and regulations governing net fishing these days. We have to protect our fishing industry – we don't want to fish out the beaches and harbours by catching fish when they are too small.)

The Smith family lived near my grandfather – next-door but one, with an old boatshed in between. They had a lovely old weatherboard home with a big verandah that was always draped with nets. They had a little backyard, too, with lots of lemon trees and apricot trees. I'll never forget those trees, especially the apricots. I've never tasted apricots like them since. They needed those lemon trees, because everybody in the district, I'm sure, procured their lemons there for the fish they bought.

In front of the cottage was a lovely old shed – right on Marine Parade, because there was no promenade then – and this old shed was piled up with nets; anchors; kerosene lamps; billy cans; frying pans; old grey blankets; buoys; old, dried-out, curiously shaped fish; and odd-

1900s

Opposite: A ferry arriving at
Watsons Bay Wharf, circa 1900

shaped fish backbones marked where sharks had
attacked the fish when they were young. There were cats
galore, and not one of them with an ounce of spare flesh.
They say fish are slimming, and these cats proved it.
They were breeding like mad, and of course suckling their
kittens, yet they lived entirely on fish. Their coats were
smooth and shining and I remember how they would
come over to you, purring with satisfaction, after a feed
of fish.

The Smith brothers lived long lives, and Grandmother
Smith must have been 100, I think, when she died. She
used to help in making and repairing the nets. Most of
their diet was fish – I know, because I used to play with
the grandchildren, Mary and Maggie Cameron. (We
remained lifelong friends.) The brothers used to stay out
all night some nights – and Grandfather did, too – looking
for schools of fish. I remember old Jack Smith at the
age of 85 up a tree on a lookout around Camp Cove, I
think it was, fell down with excitement when he saw a
large school of mullet. He broke his leg but, amazingly,
completely recovered and after a while was back on light
duties down on the beach, repairing nets and so on. I can
see him now just gazing up the Harbour, daydreaming a
little and puffing on his pipe.

*There were cats galore, and not one
of them with an ounce of spare flesh.
They say fish are slimming, and these
cats proved it.*

There was always great excitement in Watsons Bay when
the salmon season was on – and the mullet season,
too. The mullet season here in Watsons Bay was from
about March on. After a hot day the Southerly Buster,
the big cool southerly wind, would come, and that was a
signal to be on the lookout. The season went right up to
Easter. There would be hundreds of fish netted, and the
fishermen used to make a pen of netting attached to the
rails of the wharf down in the Bay and each day they'd
put all the fish they'd caught into this. They'd leave them
there till they had a big load, and then trucks from the
market would come down and the fish would be brought
up to the footpath, shovelled into boxes and taken away.
A lot of the salmon went to the fish processors for fish

1908

paste. It was exciting to us locals at the time – I suppose now no one would look. Simple but happy days. I think the fishermen received about tuppence a pound for their catch – none of them ever made a fortune, just a living. But they lived long lives and happy lives; they weren't looking for glamour.

My mother was born in Watsons Bay, as my grandfather had been, and as I was. She died at 84 after a hard working life, but she loved every moment of it. She wasn't a regular churchgoer, but she and her relatives, along with other early Watsons Bay settlers, raised the money to build St Peter's, the church on the hill. I still have the prayer book that she read nightly. It is nearly in tatters, so I have it tied together with ribbon – such a simple faith, but so loving.

I had a wonderful childhood – well, I think it was wonderful. It was spent amid everything connected with the sea. Plenty of rowing boats on the beach, fish traps, fish nets, sails. I used to have a boat – an old dinghy – and I often wonder how on earth we made it back home sailing from Nielsen Park with those stiff nor'-easters that blow across Sydney Harbour.

Grandma and Grandfather's tiny shop was pulled down (or blown down) about 1907. The Ozone Cafe was built on the same spot in 1908. A section of the original little shop still survives as part of the restaurant – we make the entrees there every day.

They used to take the window out of the tearooms because the noise from the gun turret had broken it once before.

After the Ozone was built, it was leased out for a while because my mother and father had started another business at Signal Hill, Watsons Bay, right opposite the signal station, which is about where Belah Gardens is now. I believe they had the first gas stove in Watsons Bay installed there. Next door to the signal station is a gun turret where one of the largest guns belonging to the Army was housed, and my parents told me later that when it was gun practice time they used to have to take the show window out of the tearooms because the noise the gun made when it was being fired had broken it once before.

Watsons Bay was always a popular place to visit – it was quite an enjoyable trip out by horse buggy or tram from the city. The terminus then was at Signal Hill. Mum was fond of cooking with that gas stove, and as she was an excellent cook people came back and back. Mum and Dad never made a fortune at the Signal tearooms – just enough to keep the family going, with the help of some fowls and a cow. They used to serve a hot luncheon for two shillings – mostly fish with apple pie to follow. The visitors would then go for a stroll down to Watsons Bay and visit all the beauty spots. When they climbed back up the hill to catch their conveyance to the city, they were quite welcome to call in to Mum and Dad's tearooms again and have some hot scones and a cup of tea – this time nothing to pay, just a friendly gesture, a chance to say 'Cheerio till we see you again'. You see, they had regulars, and it's good to have regular customers – that's what's kept our family business going for so many years.

Eventually, Mum and Dad went back to the Ozone, and it became a well-known Sydney eating place. We kids grew up there, helping out in all sorts of ways. Mum and Dad used to do all the cooking, and the customers could have their fish steamed, fried or grilled. With your fish you had mashed potatoes or chips and always, if you wanted it, a dish of oyster sauce as an extra, for a few pence. Of course, the sauce would be made the correct way – if the fish was steamed you'd have the juice out of that to add to your basic white sauce, then the oysters would be added to warm through for a minute or two – absolutely mouth-watering!

They presented the fish beautifully, on sizzling hot plates with plenty of parsley and lemon wedges. No side salads in those days – just the fish and potato, perfectly cooked. I always say that even after all these years we can't fry fish and chips as well as Mum did. The batter on the fish in those days was golden like corn, crisp as the thinnest biscuit wafer you can imagine. When a fork was put into the fried fish, the batter practically blew away. All the fish frying was done in pure beef dripping in those days. It had a beautiful smell as it was cooking, and I can remember putting cold dripping on my toast with pepper and salt. It was delicious. (Now, don't make a face. Plenty of people have had a snack like that – but what would my doctor think!) Really, in my opinion, there is nothing to beat pure beef dripping for baking or frying and none of the oils we use today impart that special flavour to the food.

The Ozone Cafe had two floors. The ground floor was the oyster room, and I can clearly remember its beautiful marble tabletops with their wrought-iron stands – so many of them – and plenty of flowers in jars all round the room. Each day the lino was freshly polished. Each day, too, pepper and salt shakers and vinegar jars had to be filled up. Every marble table had its own bottle of black sauce (Worcestershire sauce), with a serviette tied around the bottle.

The menu at Ozone was always written freshly every day and placed in a brass container outside the entrance door.

The oysters were kept up the back in the fish room. This had a concrete floor and was gauzed in with a wire door. The fish ice chests were kept there. With every order of oysters you had to rush, and I mean rush, up the stairs from the bottom dining room out to the fish room and open the oysters yourself. Just as well we didn't have the crowds to serve that we have nowadays! The wet bags had to be taken off the oysters and, using Grandfather's oyster opener, you set to work. It was a wonderful oyster opener – Grandfather made it himself. I never did know what became of it, and nor did Mum. It should have been patented – would have made a fortune for us. Mum always warned us to be careful, with the oysters at ten shillings a bag. We were told not to waste them by sticking the knife into them while we were opening them. And, of course, not to eat any ourselves.

The top dining room of our restaurant was homely, with lovely round tables with white tablecloths, each table with an old-fashioned elegant cruet and a little vase of flowers, mostly wildflowers that Grandfather used to get from the bush. I used to gather flannel flowers for the restaurant myself, and red-tipped gum from parks nearby.

The menu at Ozone was always written freshly every day and placed in a brass container outside the entrance door. I wonder why they bothered – prices didn't fluctuate and the fish was practically the same every day. Of course, mullet predominated when the season was on, and let me tell you now it was popular and really delicious.

Watsons Bay was a very popular place to visit by ferry in those days, as it had been in my grandparents' time. Visitors would catch the ferry from Circular Quay, and

on the way to the Bay the ferry would call at Garden Island, then Nielsen Park wharf, then it would come round Bottle'n'Glass (a pleasant picnic area there). On it would go to Parsley Bay wharf, then pass the suspension bridge across Parsley Bay and continue to Central Wharf, the wharf that brought you up to the Crescent in Vaucluse. A few hundred yards on from Central Wharf was the Watsons Bay wharf. The wharf was picturesque with its old-fashioned waiting shed. It was a favourite fishing spot, and there would always be a scurry to pull your line in quickly just as the ferry came pounding in. Gosh, there must have been a lot of big ones got away there.

In summer, people would bring their swimsuits and have a swim in the baths. Not many people swam at Camp Cove or Lady Jane in those days – probably frightened of sharks. We kids used to swim out in front of the restaurant. I guess we were lucky. The old Watsons Bay wharf waiting shed was pulled down, and in its place stand the Sydney Big Game Fishing Association clubrooms. They weigh the sharks and marlin at the weighing platform there. It was a great loss to the local environment when that old shed was taken away, both because it was a historic building and because of its unusual design. Perhaps Urban Transport thought that the ferry would never again come to Watsons Bay . . .

Down near the wharf at one time there was a huge old tree, and under this tree the line and net fishermen used to spread their fish out on a table to sell. After you bought it, you either cleaned it yourself or asked the fishermen to do it for you. Fish was fairly plentiful then, and you could buy beautiful big deep-sea flathead, snapper, huge jewfish, bream, garfish and lots of other fish there, including some choice pig fish. Pig fish has succulent white flesh, and mostly the fishermen would keep these for themselves, unless you were a special customer. Often the day's catch of fish would be a mixed lot, but it was always worth buying. There were also plenty of mussels and oysters for the taking on the rocks around the Bay and the other Harbour bays. The oysters were small and strong in flavour but most popular, and many a bottle was collected and raffled at the local hotel over the years.

The Ozone Cafe was closed during the Depression, but as it was my parents' home it remained in the family. Jack and I lived there with our four sons for many years.

1948

Above: Jack and me on the day we reopened my family's old restaurant, the Ozone Cafe, 28 March 1948

I had met Jack on a blind date at a dinner dance in Watsons Bay in 1929 and we married a year later. Our sons followed – Peter in 1932, John in 1934, Michael in 1937 and Timothy in 1939, the day the Second World War was declared. Then, when my husband returned from the Second World War, I felt I wanted to reopen the business. The New South Wales Government had an Army rehabilitation programme which made loans available to ex-servicemen to help them get started again. They refused permission for our loan, saying that the little old 'cafe' was too bad a risk. So Mum came to our rescue with the £60 it took us to equip ourselves, and we were in business again. The fish was reasonably plentiful, and we could buy locally. (This is, of course, illegal now.) The fish meal was three shillings and sixpence, with bread and butter, a pot of tea and hot scones and jam thrown in. Mum made the scones and the jam and also her father's famous fish soup.

There were still lots of fishermen living in Watsons Bay at that time and Hedley Tinker was still net fishing, taking over from his old relatives, the Smiths. Bill Love was a well-known and much respected fisherman in the Bay then. He was the late Sam Hordern's boatman on his big game cruiser, and in those days they really caught the big sharks. Then there were the Abbott brothers, Jim Chapman and Jack Farrell – Bay fishermen, who also used a lot of set lines and caught the most beautiful snapper. I used to go down to the boats and buy for the cafe, at the same time admiring these beautiful creatures from the sea. Snapper, to me, are one of the most outstanding fish that swim in our waters, with their beautiful shades of pink and those clear blue eyes and the shining iridescent scales on their big frames. Some of them, as they get older, have a big hump on the top part of their spine or backbone – I believe that is a guide to their age. Sounds as if I am describing a beauty competition. Well, they are beauties to us and anyone else that partakes of them.

It was hard work, getting started again. I used to clean fish in the morning out in the garden, and then cook it for the lunchtime crowd. It was always a rush, but it was such a good time, too. The business has grown so now – from one little cafe to a chain of restaurants. It makes you smile to think how the 'bad risk' has turned out!

I believe we've done well because we've always stuck to the one principle that Mum followed in her time: perfect fresh fish, cooked and served simply but well – and plenty of it! Our menu still says that there is no charge for an extra portion of fish, if you still happen to be hungry.

One happy part of reopening the restaurant in 1948 was the good wishes of our friends in the Bay, accompanied by the words, 'We'll give you a hand very willingly until you can afford to employ staff,' and they did. The first weekend in the Easter season – a couple of weeks after we opened – an old friend of my parents, John (Uncle John) Fitzpatrick, who at that time was living at Westmead, came to see us. 'I've got my apron with me,' he said, 'and I'm going to do the washing-up on the weekends.' And he did – he helped us so much for three years.

John Fitzpatrick had come to Australia as a young man from Dublin in 1907, on the SS *Medic*. (The fare was £17 in those days.) He answered an advertisement my father had put in the *Herald* for a handyman who could milk a cow, tend to the kitchen and help in the Signal tearooms. When my mother opened the door to the handsome young Irishman, complete with Donga tweeds, cap and cane – and, of course, the voice and charm to match – she had to tell him that she had given

We've always stuck to the one principle: perfect fresh fish, cooked and served simply but well — and plenty of it!

the job to another young man earlier in the day. John's reply was: 'Here, give him this half-crown, engage me, and you will not be sorry.' So that Irish charm brought John Fitzpatrick into our life, and he later married my mother's girlfriend, beautiful Emily Kennedy.

My mother often told me this story of her and Dad's early days, and of how busy they were at the tearooms when the first American fleet ever to visit Sydney arrived in 1908. People walked out from Sydney to the Gap, if they couldn't get onto one of the early trams, to see the ships come through the Heads and into Sydney Harbour. It must have been quite a night and a day.

Many thanks to all the customers who have supported us over all these years. I know at times you have been inconvenienced – when the weather has been bad,

1968

Left to right: Tim, Michael, Jack, Alice, Peter and John

there are seafood shortages, and then when the holiday season is on, service is not always as good as we would like. But we thank you sincerely for 'sticking with us'.

When I look back over the years to the time after the war when my husband returned once again to civilian life and we reopened my parents' little cafe on the beach, it's hard to believe we have come so far. Whatever parents do, it's never too much if it's of benefit to them and their children. They were happy days, and oh, how I wish we were just beginning it all again!

My youngest son, Tim, has written about growing up at the old Ozone Cafe. It goes like this:

'Did Ya?' by Tim Doyle

An inward flow of memories comes to me like the tide on a rising sea. My own personal thoughts are hidden very deeply in a spot in my brain that has become a sacred storage. You have to find solitude to be able to relive memories like these.

Did you have a billycart like I did when I was a kid? I collected coke and driftwood, filled my old odd-wheeled 'cart' and went around the Bay floggin' it to all those people who had a fuel stove or fireplace. Did you ever boil periwinkles around the creek, the creek that is between the rocks and the sea at Camp Cove, Watsons Bay? Then, when the periwinkles were cooked, you had to rush home along the beachfront to Mum and get some pins to hook them out of their shells. I did. Did you ever look, or stare, and think about the hard flat feet and huge toes of the fishermen who lived along the Bay and had their feet in the water as they were dragging up the nets? The skin was peeling and their toenails had become so very long and hard. Honest hard-working feet that had walked their way over oysters, glass, shell grit, etc, etc, and had tangled in seaweed that housed the remains of fish skeletons. Feet that could stand the burning-hot sands but could not bear the pain of having to wear boots, on the rare occasion when they had to.

Did you ever really smell the old clothes that lie in a heap in an old boatshed, yours for the taking when sorely needed? There were Army greatcoats and old suit pants, both at some time wet through with sea spray and sand, home to every old stray dog, every cat and her kittens. Strange nowadays, perhaps, but I remember that smell and can remember many fishermen picking up a coat from that same heap as they hired a boat. 'Can I have a lend of this? It may blow up a bit of rain. Dark cloud in the South.'

Did you ever get chased by that lovable old salt that us kids knew wouldn't harm you? He always pretended to be after Rollo and me, then he would laugh like mad when he saw us running as fast as we could. You see, he was a Negro and the story went that he jumped ship in Sydney Harbour and settled around the shores of Watsons Bay. What an eye he had for beauty.

Did you ever lift the floorboards in the rowboats, looking and hoping for a find of sinkers and hooks? Did you ever catch a crab with a nail hammered into a broom handle? Or get an 'ocky' and lower it down to the bottom of the sea because you spotted a fisherman's knife that had been dropped in?

Did you ever send a dog home after he had followed you, then see him slink away as if his mate had let him down, then feel sorry and call him back and see his tail really get to work, his ears prick as he came bouncing back to you, mates again? Like what we all want to be, wanted.

Did ya, too? Ya did.

Watsons Bay gets more beautiful to me every hour, every minute.

Sydney Harbour, and that gentle lap of the waves onto the beach, making a tinkling sound as they draw back, washing lightly over the shell grit is music to my ears, just as it was when I was a child sleeping in the front room of what is now the restaurant. I can never forget such a simple, happy memory!

I found an interesting item not so long ago in an old book about Sydney Town, together with a photograph of the Sydney Fish Markets in 1909. 'Fish is about the dearest thing one can buy,' a journalist wrote at the time. He went on to say that this was one of the most extraordinary features of Sydney's food supply, although the ocean was at the city's very door. 'The cost of fish is an eye-opener, and for citizens of limited means a fish meal becomes a luxury.' So perhaps things haven't changed as much as we sometimes think!

Something else that hasn't changed much is the recipe for succeeding in business. I came across the following advice in a turn-of-the-century newspaper I found among my late father's possessions. I hope you enjoy it as much as I did.

How to Prosper in Business

In the first place, make up your mind to accomplish whatever you undertake; decide upon some particular employment, persevere in it. All difficulties are overcome by diligence and assiduity. Be not afraid to work with your hands, and diligently too.

'A cat in gloves catches no mice.'

'He who remains in the mill grinds; not he who goes and comes.'

Attend to your own business; never trust to anyone else: 'A pot that belongs to too many is ill stirred and worse boiled.'

Be frugal: 'That which will not make a pot will make a pot-lid.'

'Save the pence, and the pounds will take care of themselves.'

Be abstemious: 'Who dainties love shall beggars prove.'

Rise early: 'The sleepy fox catches no poultry.'

'Plough deep while sluggards sleep, and you will have corn to sell and to keep.'

Treat everyone with respect and civility: 'Everything is gained and nothing is lost by courtesy.'

'Good manners ensure success.'

Never anticipate wealth from any other source than labour – especially never place dependence upon becoming the possessor of an inheritance: 'He who waits for dead men's shoes may have to go a long time barefoot.'

'He who runs after a shadow hath a wearisome race.'

Above all things, never despair – God is where He was; He helps those who trust in Him.

Read not books alone, but men; and chiefly be careful to read thyself.

With a gift the miser meet;
Proud men with obeisance greet;
Women's silly fancies soothe;
Give wise men their due
— the truth.

Hitopadesa

*W*ho's who in the family business nowadays? Peter, our eldest son, is in charge of Doyles on the Beach at Watsons Bay. He is very 'clued up' about Australian fish and seafood, and served with the then Sydney Fish Marketing Authority for many of his young years as a fishing inspector on the north coast of New South Wales. It was the love of fishing that made him choose this particular job, and an outside one at that. He was a popular kind of a fishing inspector, confiscated a few nets and undersized fish in his time. (I must admit I've done a bit of illegal-size fishing myself. It's that feel of the bream when it plays with the bait and then you finally hook it. It feels much bigger than it really is when you are pulling it in, and when you land it you think, 'I'll have it for breakfast. I'll fry it whole and watch the bones.' It was always very nice for breakfast, too.) His eldest son, Peter Jnr, is now managing Doyles on the Beach. Peter Jnr is an excellent cook and has spent time in Japan and other overseas countries noting the dishes visitors to Australia will want to find here. For instance, you will now find sashimi on our menu (and in this book) — a far cry from when Jack and I, and my mother and grandparents before us, just cooked local fish and chips!

What wonderful days — when fish nets were thrown into the water from the beach in front of our cafe.

I recently came across the cashbook Jack and I kept in 1948. Here are some entries for 11 April: 'weekly milk, 11s 5d; baker 8s; groceries for weekend trading 15s; extra milk 4d and a lettuce etc. [the etc. was probably parsley] 1s 5½d [I must have had to send one of our children for those]; fish £2; plain flour [for batter] 2s.' What wonderful days — when fish nets were thrown into the water from the beach in front of our cafe and two healthy elderly fishermen slowly pulled them in, while a third man rowing a dinghy helped to keep the net full of fish together. Oh, those memories of getting started, and that bookkeeping!

John, our second son, and his wife, Barbara used to manage our beautiful waterfront hotel and beer garden at Watsons Bay before John retired.

Michael, our third son, is very involved with our Fisherman's Wharf Restaurant at Watsons Bay and is also

1984

Christopher Doyle, Jack Doyle, Peter Doyle Sr, Peter Doyle and Michael Doyle Jr.

Doyles restaurants today

On the map:
- North Head
- South Head
- **1** Watsons Bay
- Sydney Harbour
- Circular Quay **3**
- Darling Harbour
- Rose Bay
- Tasman Sea
- **2** Blackwattle Bay

1

Doyles on the Beach, Watsons Bay

On this, our original site, we opened Australia's first seafood restaurant in 1885. Ever since, it has been family owned and operated for over 5 generations.

**Doyles on the Beach,
11 Marine Parade,
Watsons Bay, Sydney
Phone: (02) 9337 2007**

Doyles Fishermans Wharf, Watsons Bay

Situated over the water, the restaurant is open seven days a week. You can dine inside or al fresco and you will still be able to enjoy the fabulous views of Watsons Bay and the city skyline. Live lobsters and mud crabs are a feature of the menu here. The seafood take-away section offers generous helpings of very affordable seafood, as well as coffee, cold drinks and ice creams.

**Doyles Fishermans Wharf,
Watsons Bay Wharf, Sydney
Phone: (02) 9337 1572**

Doyles Palace Hotel, Watsons Bay

Situated right on the Harbour's edge, with views across Sydney Harbour to the dramatic backdrop of the city skyline, the hotel seems a million miles from care. Watsons Bay is located 12 kilometres from the city centre and has daily ferry services to Circular Quay. For our guests we can arrange a preferential reservation for you to dine with us at our harbourfront restaurants or our famous beer garden at Watsons Bay or catch the ferry to our Circular Quay restaurant.

**Doyles Palace Hotel,
Military Road, Watsons Bay,
Sydney
Phone: (02) 9337 5444**

2

Doyles Bistro at the Fish Markets

Situated right In the heart of the Sydney Fish Markets at Pyrmont, our bistro has great views over Blackwattle Bay. It's the best value seafood in town. You can select your own lunch from our classic fish and chips through to scallops, prawns, or even lobster. And everything is cooked fresh at market prices. Travel by car, bus or the Sydney Light Rail Service.

**Doyles Bistro at the Fish Markets.
Gipps Street, Pyrmont, Sydney
Phone: (02) 9552 4339**

3

Doyles at the Quay

We're located at the Harbour Bridge end of the International Overseas Shipping Terminal at Circular Quay. Our gourmet seafood restaurant is directly opposite the Sydney Opera House, with breathtaking views of the Harbour. As one critic said; 'Superior seafood on the choicest piece of real estate in the world.'

**Doyles at the Quay,
Overseas Terminal,
Circular Quay, Sydney
Phone: (02) 9252 3400**

the accountant for our entire business. His eldest son, Jim, now manages the restaurant, and like his father is an excellent cook. Jim's brother, David, is the manager of our bistro and bottle shop at the Sydney Fish Markets at Pyrmont, where we have our own fish-cleaning rooms. We have had a long association with this outlet at the markets – you'll always find a Doyle down there cleaning fish or serving. I can honestly say that our fish is the freshest and best variety obtainable – and then perfectly filleted. We certainly have a battle getting supplies at times, though, and have to make frequent interstate trips to make sure that the fish and other seafoods we want are available.

Some things — places, sunrise, sunset, full moons — are just as beautiful as ever. It's a matter of taking the time to stop, look and listen.

Our newest restaurant at Circular Quay, Doyles at the Quay, is another glorious spot, where you can feast outdoors while feasting your eyes on the Opera House sails, gleaming like the scales of those beautiful, big fresh snapper I wrote about earlier, and watching the water traffic – ferries, luxury cruisers, a paddlewheeler – churning up the Harbour. All reflected in a blue sky by day, and at night – fairyland.

I remember when I was a child coming home to Watsons Bay in the evening with my mother from Jetty No. 1, in the old ferry *Vaucluse*, and watching one of the first neon signs in Sydney. It was a Penfolds sign showing a bottle pouring out a glass of red wine. What a lasting impression that made on me – as I write this I have a tear in my eye that those early days will never come back. (At my age, truly, it's memories that keep you going. Sometimes I wake up with a start, thinking, 'I can smell the potatoes burning. Time to fry the fish.')

Our family is growing. We have twenty grandchildren – fourteen of whom work in the family business – and now fifteen great-grandchildren.

Unfortunately my husband Jack has passed away, but I still think it's important to keep going even if it means pushing myself. I still keep a daily diary. I like to cook and probably spend about four hours a day in my kitchen. Every day I pass the house where I was born, and I think what a place to have been born – Watsons Bay, the spot the good Lord worked on overtime (and with no penalty rates). Some things – places, sunrise, sunset, full moons – are just as beautiful as ever. It's a matter of taking the time to stop, look and listen.

Whenever I sign copies of my book for people, as I often do, I always say, 'Hope you enjoy the recipes in this, my cookbook. It's the best I could do.' I hope all my readers enjoy them.

Thank you for buying this book – someone tonight will sleep much more comfortably than last night, thanks to the Sydney City Mission.

Sincerely, Alice Doyle

The Doyle family today. Opposite page: Lewis Doyle (Sitting on the sand), then, clockwise: Peter Doyle OAM, James Doyle, Sarfraz Khan, Peter Doyle AM (in hat), Robyn Doyle, Gayle Doyle, Jack Doyle, Christopher Doyle and Michael Doyle Jr. This page: Hunter Doyle and Ruby Doyle (playing in the sand), Ben Doyle with Jasper Doyle on lap, John Doyle, Lisa Doyle, Elizabeth Doyle, Patrick Kelton, Michael Doyle, Martin Hieber and David Doyle.

Before You Start

In Praise of Fish

Seafoods on the average are the most digestible of foods and ideally adapted for bodily assimilation by humans. No poor fish ever gets so tough as some of those range steers you run into.

Did you know that man cannot exist for three months in perfect health without the essentials contained in seafoods? Without charging you any more per pound, fish assimilate these essential chemicals from the sea, and you know what you have to pay in the chemist's for substitute drugs.

Fish extract iodine from the sea to prevent you contracting goitre; oysters extract copper from the sea to enrich your bloodstream. Fish is also a good source of calcium, phosphorus and iron to keep your bones and flesh intact, even fluorine and arsenic for your fingernails, as well as vitamins you require from A to D.

We cannot divulge all the other benefits you derive, or fishermen would want more for their fish and the Government would impose a tax on food with such a high drug content.

You had better rush out right now and buy yourself some fish. Brother! You need it!

from *The Fisheries Newsletter*, August 1956

Buying & Keeping Fish

The following information was kindly provided by the Sydney Fish Market.

How Much to Buy?

Whole fish 1 kg (about 2 lb) Serves 2

Whole fish, gutted, with head, fins and tail removed 450 g–500 g (about 1 lb) Serves 2

Steaks or cutlets 500 g (1 lb) Serves 2–3

Skinned fillets 500 g (1 lb) Serves 3–4

Guide to Quality

Fresh whole fish have bright, full eyes and gills that are pink-red and have a pleasant sea smell. The flesh is elastic, springing back when gently pressed.

How Long to Keep

Fresh fish should be used as soon as possible after purchase. It will keep in the refrigerator for 2–3 days. Keep fish on a plate covered with waxed paper, foil or plastic in the coldest part of the refrigerator.

Frozen Fish

Whole fish can be frozen for up to 6 months as long as the temperature of your freezer is -18°C or less. Oily fish, fillets and cutlets will keep for 3 months.

Make sure fish is scaled, gutted, gilled and rinsed before freezing.

Once frozen fish is thawed, it deteriorates at a faster rate than fresh fish, so use immediately. Never refreeze thawed fish.

Breaded fish – scallops, fish fingers and fillets – should never be thawed before cooking.

Some Popular Table Fish & Seafood

Abalone

Several species of abalone are found in Australia. The meat of the abalone is very firm and has a unique flavour and texture. Live abalone can be stored in the refrigerator for 2–3 days.

Balmain Bugs

Balmain bugs are available all year round. Moreton Bay bugs, found in Queensland are very similar. Bugs are sold whole cooked or raw. They can be stored in the refrigerator for up to 3 days in an airtight container.

Barramundi or Giant Perch

Considered by many to be Australia's top eating fish because of its moist, flavoursome, well-textured flesh. Many lesser species are sometimes misrepresented as barramundi.

Bream

A delicate table fish, usually bought in small fillets.

Coral Trout and Cod

These two magnificent table fish, occasionally confused with each other, compete for the honour of premium fish of the Great Barrier Reef.

Crab

There are three types of crabs usually found in the markets – the blue swimmer, the mud crab and the spanner crab. Crabs are usually sold whole either cooked or raw. Live mud crabs should be kept in a wet hessian bag in a cool place. Otherwise, crabs can be stored in the refrigerator for up to 3 days.

Crayfish (Lobster)

Also called rock lobster. It is considered a gastronomic delight the world over. The flesh is white, firm and sweet, with a distinctive flavour all its own.

Flathead

The flesh of the tiger flathead is white, tender and flavoursome. It never reaches a size that makes it coarse or tough as some other flathead species sometimes do. The river flathead ranks high as a food fish. Although the flesh is a little dry, it is white, firm and has a good flavour. The sand flathead is similar in taste and texture to the tiger.

Gemfish, Hake or King Barracouta

A fish of excellent quality; the flesh has a good texture. It has a pleasant though slightly more pronounced flavour than most Australian fish. A tasty smoked product has been developed.

Jewfish or Mulloway

Young jewfish of 1–3 kg (2¼ lb–6¾ lb) are excellent eating. In fish below the length of 46 cm (18½ in), the flesh tends to be soft and mushy. The flesh of large mulloway becomes flaky, with a tendency to coarseness and loss of flavour.

John Dory

Considered a delicacy of the sea. A prominent black spot on each side is said to represent the imprints of St Peter's thumb and first finger, made as he took a piece of money from the fish's mouth. The flesh is firm, white and tender, with a deliciously succulent flavour.

Leatherjacket

Good eating fish with delicate white flesh. Best cooked whole.

Mirror Dory or Silver Dory

A tasty fish with firm, white flesh. Usually an economical buy.

Morwong or Sea Bream

A good eating fish similar to bream but a little stronger in flavour.

Mullet

A much-maligned fish because it occasionally has an 'earthy' flavour. If prepared and cooked correctly, this is a fish of exceptionally good quality. The flavour is rich and the flesh always tender, except for a short period after spawning when the flesh darkens.

Murray Cod

A gourmet's delight and the most delicious of Australia's inland freshwater fish. It has white, firm flesh of good quality, and can be cooked in many ways.

Mussels

Two types of mussel are commonly available – blue and the New Zealand greenlip. Blue mussels should be tightly closed or snap closed when touched. The greenlip mussel can be open. Mussels can be stored for up to 3 days in the refrigerator. Discard any damaged mussels. Scrub and remove the beard before cooking.

Octopus

Octopus has eight tentacles and are available in varying sizes. Most small octopus found in the market have been tenderised. You may find large octopus will need long slow cooking to tenderise them. Octopus can be stored in the refrigerator for up to 2 days. Don't forget to remove the head and clean out the gut and the beak before cooking. The head and the body can be eaten.

Oysters

Oysters can be purchased unopened, opened and displayed on the half shell or in jars. They should be plump with a rich creamy colour. They should have a pleasant sea smell. Keepability of oysters varies so check with your fishmonger. Sydney rock oysters have a worldwide reputation for quality and taste.

Prawns

The biggest and best-known of Australian prawns are king prawns (eastern and western). They are delicious to eat. Other species include brown, tiger and banana prawns. Smaller school and greentail prawns are common as bait for anglers but are good eating. A nuisance to peel, but well worth the effort – the flesh is sweet and succulent.

Red Emperor

An excellent food fish of fine flavour and firm texture, with striking colouration.

Redfish or Nannygai

Has white, tender, sweetly succulent flesh which flakes easily from the bones.

Salmon (Atlantic)

Many of the salmon in the fish market are farmed. Salmon is available whole, filleted or in cutlet form. Its distinctive orange flesh is much prized for its wonderful flavour.

Scallops

The small, sweet meats of these shellfish are suitable for a wide range of dishes.

Shark

Gummy and school shark are the main species marketed. Sold as flake in Victoria and as shark (and many other names) in other States/Territories. Its flesh is boneless and flaky, of good texture but distinct flavour. Popular in the fish and chip trade.

Snapper

Probably the best-known commercial fish and universally popular for eating. Its flesh is white, firm and tasty, though really big fish can be a little coarse and dry.

Spanish Mackerel

The slightly dry, well-flavoured, firm-textured flesh is usually marketed in cutlet form and is excellent for a wide variety of baked, barbecued or marinated fish dishes.

Squid (Calamari)

Soft-bodied molluscs sold fresh or frozen; whole, in tubes or cut into rings. Clean and gut whole squid before storing. They can be kept in the refrigerator for up to 3 days.

Tuna

Tuna is sold mainly in steaks. Sashimi tuna is usually sold separately to the tuna steaks. You can keep tuna in the refrigerator for up to 3 days. It is best cooked rare.

West Australian Jewfish or Dhu

Should not be confused with the mulloway jewfish of the eastern States. It is a reef fish related to the pearl perch and, like it, is excellent for eating. The flesh is beautifully white, and always tender, with a delicate flavour.

Whiting

The spotted, King George or South Australian whiting is regarded by many southerners as the only table fish. Its white, fine-textured flesh has a delicate, slightly sweet flavour.

Anzac Bridge as the sun is rising

Availability: When and Where

VARIETY	NT	QLD	NSW	VIC	TAS	SA	WA
Barramundi *(giant perch)*	**	Nov-Mar	-	-	-	-	Apr-Nov
Bream *black*	-	Jun	**	**	-	-	**
Bream *silver*	-	-	May-Jun	-	-	-	-
Cod *Murray*	-	-	**	Jan-Oct	-	Dec-Aug	-
Crab *mud*	**	Feb-Apr	Nov-Feb	-	-	-	**
Crab *sand*	-	Nov-Mar	**	-	-	-	Jan-Mar
Flathead *river (black)*	-	May-Jul	**	**	-	-	Jan-Aug
Flathead *sand*	-	May-Jul	Jan-Mar	**	**	**	-
Flathead *tiger*	-	-	Jan-Mar	**	**	-	-
Gemfish *(hake, king barracouta)*	-	-	Jul-Aug	Mar-Jun	-	-	-
Jewfish *(mulloway)*	**	Apr-May	Mar-Apr	-	-	Nov-May	Aug-Apr
Jewfish *Westralian (dhu)*	-	-	-	-	-	-	**
John Dory	-	*	Feb-Apr	*	**	-	-
Kingfish *yellowtail*	-	Jun	Jan-Mar	**	-	Jan-Mar	-
Leatherjacket *ocean*	-	-	Feb-Apr	**	**	**	**
Leatherjacket *rough (yellow)*	-	-	**	-	-	**	Mar-Jun
Lobster *rock*	-	-	Jul-Aug	**	Nov-Aug	Nov-Sep	Nov-Aug
Mackerel *Spanish*	**	Oct-Dec	**	-	-	-	Jul-Oct
Morwong *(sea bream)*	-	-	Apr-Jul	**	**	-	Dec-Aug
Mullet	-	Apr-Jul	Feb-Apr	**	**	**	Jan-Mar

VARIETY	NT	QLD	NSW	VIC	TAS	SA	WA
Oysters Sydney rock	-	**	**	**	-	-	Apr-Nov
Perch pearl	-	Apr-Jul	**	-	-	-	-
Prawns banana	-	Feb-Jun	-	-	-	-	-
Prawns bay	-	Dec-Apr	-	-	-	-	-
Prawns king	Jun-Dec	Nov-Sep	**	**	-	**	Mar-Sep
Prawns school	-	Feb-Apr	Nov-Mar	**	-	-	Dec-Apr
Prawns tiger	-	May-Sep	-	-	-	-	-
Red emperor	-	Mar-Jul	-	-	-	-	-
Redfish (nannygai)	-	-	May-Jun	**	-	-	Dec-Aug
Red sweetlip	-	Mar-Jul	-	-	-	-	-
Salmon Australian	-	-	**	**	**	**	Feb-May
Scallops sea	-	Sep-Mar	*	**	May-Nov	May-Jul	Mar-Sep
Shark (flake)	**	*	**	**	**	**	Feb-Sep
Snapper	-	Apr-Jul	May-Jun	**	-	**	Apr-Sep
Squid	Jun-Dec	Feb-Apr	**	**	Nov-Feb	**	**
Trevally	**	*	**	**	**	-	Feb-Jul
Trout coral	-	Mar-Jul	-	-	-	-	-
Tuna	-	Feb-May	**	May-Jun	Jan-Jun	Jan-Apr	Feb-Aug
Whiting sand	-	May-Aug	**	**	-	-	Jul-Nov
Whiting King George	-	-	**	**	**	**	Mar-Aug

**available all year
* available occasionally or in small quantities
- not available

Soups, Starters

& Dips

Soups & Chowders

Do you know just how many delicious and nourishing meals can be made from the backbones and the heads of fish? Well, the imaginative cook can make the most wonderful dishes, and a good fish supplier can become one of the cook's best friends. What better or more nourishing food for the family — especially when served with the flair of the professional with vegetables grated finely, toasted sippets, Melba toast, cheese and luscious cream.

But please don't say to your guests or to your family: 'Have some fish soup.' Give it a fancy name: 'We are having seafood bisque tonight.' And don't forget to have lashings of crusty bread, garlic bread or bruschetta, and salt and freshly ground pepper on the table.

Fish Stock

There will be times when you are cooking and you will have the small fish you or the kids have caught, or you have filleted a big snapper that was won in one of those pub raffles. Or, if you're lucky, the prawn glut is on and you are flat out peeling to make some curried prawns or garlic prawns. With these little fish, snapper bones or heads, or the prawn shells if available, you can make stock for some of your seafood dishes. Don't use small-boned fish for stock as it is too hard to strain the bones out.

This will be a strong-flavoured stock with body. This is the basic recipe. To this, you can also add any of the following: carrot, celery, leek, onion, parsley and peppercorns. Vary the number of skeletons and the amount of water to make the amount of stock you need.

3 fish skeletons, including well-scaled heads

1 teaspoon salt

water

Wash fish pieces thoroughly and put in a heavy saucepan or stewpan. Add salt and fill the pan with water. Bring to a boil, then simmer strongly for 1 hour. If the bones and heads are large and you have a fair amount, cook longer.

If you want to keep some of the flesh from the heads and bones, take them out after they have been cooking for ½ hour and put the flesh aside. Put the remains back in the pot and continue cooking.

Strain stock carefully through a fine strainer or sieve making sure you do not let any bone, particle of shell, or scale through.

When cold, refrigerate the stock until needed. After a day the stock will be a jelly. You now have the basic foundation for any soup or seafood dishes you want to create.

If you make stock a couple of days before you are going to use it, omit salt. In any case, keep stock no longer than 2 days (unless, of course, you freeze it).

Makes enough for 8 people

Cream of Snapper Soup

John Doyle's speciality! Get those tastebuds working for this one. Ask yourself: 'Is there something missing?' Add more anchovy essence or seasoning if you like, but go easy to keep that fish flavour.

8 cups fish stock made using
    snapper bones and head

2 large potatoes, peeled and diced

2 large brown onions, peeled and finely chopped

4 stalks celery, finely chopped

½ cup rice or sago

1 teaspoon dried basil

4 drops Tabasco sauce

1 or 2 bay leaves, to taste

1 teaspoon salt

pepper

½ cup plain flour

1 cup milk (more may be needed)

2 teaspoons curry powder (optional)

2 teaspoons anchovy sauce

2 or 3 large carrots, grated

chopped parsley, to garnish

Heat the fish stock, add the potatoes, onions, celery, rice, basil, Tabasco sauce, bay leaves, salt and pepper. Cook for ½ hour, then thicken with plain flour mixed to a smooth paste with the cup of milk. Add the curry powder if you're using it.

Let the flour cook through the mixture until you cannot taste it. Add anchovy sauce, stir in well, and a few minutes before the soup is ready, put in the grated carrot. Garnish with parsley.

Serve this soup boiling hot with sippets of bruschetta or dry toast.

Serves 8

This is an excellent light soup. Omit the flour if you wish to put in more vegetables. Just before serving, if desired, you can add the fish you picked from the bones and heads when you were making your fish stock.

Crab Bisque

My thanks to Janine Haines, former leader of the Australian Democrats, for this rather special soup.

4 blue swimmer crabs, uncooked

8 cups water

1 onion, chopped

60 g (2 oz) butter

½ cup dry white wine

¼ cup brandy

2 medium tomatoes, peeled, deseeded and chopped

¼ cup uncooked white rice

2 teaspoons tomato paste

2 egg yolks, beaten

½ cup cream

1 or 2 tablespoons fresh chopped dill

freshly ground black pepper

sour cream (optional)

Remove meat from crab shells, discarding any grey tissue. Chop any large chunks of crabmeat into smaller pieces. Refrigerate the crabmeat until ready to use.

To make crab stock, place washed shells in a large saucepan with 8 cups water. Bring to boil and simmer, uncovered, for 30 minutes. Strain and reserve stock. (Discard the shells well away from the neighbourhood cats!)

Cook onion in butter in a large saucepan. When onion is soft, add wine, brandy and stock. Bring to boil and add tomatoes, rice and tomato paste. Simmer, uncovered, for 20 minutes.

Combine beaten egg yolks with cream and add to soup. Blend to a smooth consistency. Add crabmeat, fresh dill and some freshly ground black pepper. Reheat, but do not boil.

Serve with a dollop of sour cream if desired.

Serves 6

Oyster Soup

This is a very old recipe and full of the good things needed for a delicious, nourishing soup.
It's work, but worth the effort for all the praise you'll receive.

fish bones for stock

3 cups milk

2 cups fish stock (recipe page 41) or water

1 carrot, sliced

1 small brown onion, chopped

2 bay leaves

pinch dried basil

4 peppercorns

salt, to taste

60 g (2 oz) butter

1 tablespoon flour

2 egg yolks, beaten

1 cup cream

2 dozen oysters on the shell or bottled

few drops Tabasco sauce

1 teaspoon Worcestershire sauce

finely chopped parsley, to garnish

If you use bottled oysters, discard the water they are in and rinse before using.

Cut fish bones into small pieces. Put them in a saucepan with milk, prepared fish stock or water, carrot, onion, bay leaves, basil, peppercorns and salt. Simmer gently for ½ hour. Strain. Discard bones, vegetables and seasonings.

Melt the butter in a pan, stir in the flour to make a smooth paste. Add the strained fish stock, stir until boiling ensuring there are no flour lumps. Cook for 3 to 5 minutes.

Beat the egg yolks and cream together. Strain into the soup and stir for a few minutes, taking care that the soup does not boil. Carefully place oysters (off the shell) in, add Tabasco sauce and Worcestershire sauce. Serve immediately, so that the oysters are just warmed through.

For a finishing touch, garnish with parsley and serve with bruschetta.

Serves 4

Rich Vegetable Fish Chowder

You can also add prawns, crayfish or crabs to this dish to make it taste even better!

½ cup olive oil or polyunsaturated margarine or butter

1 brown onion, chopped

2 large sticks celery, chopped

1 capsicum, chopped

1 parsnip, chopped

1 carrot, chopped

½ leek, chopped

½ bunch green onions (scallions), chopped

1 clove garlic, finely chopped

½ teaspoon dried dill

½ cup chopped fresh basil

pinch nutmeg

dash Tabasco sauce

salt and pepper

1 egg, beaten

1 tablespoon cream

1 kg (2 lb) or more thick fish (gemfish, jewfish, cod and so on) filleted, boned and skinned, and cut into small portions

plain flour

Sao biscuit crumbs

1 cup moselle or fish stock (recipe page 41) sweetened with a little sugar

chopped parsley, to garnish

paprika, to garnish

Place ¼ cup oil in a very large pan and heat. Add vegetables and simmer slowly; add all seasonings and stir, turning vegetables over and over till mixed in. This will take about 15 minutes of slow cooking. Remove vegetables and reserve until later.

Beat egg and cream together. Coat fillets of fish with egg and cream mixture. Flour the fish, then dip in biscuit crumbs. Gently fry in remaining oil until fish is cooked, about 7 to 8 minutes, depending on thickness of fish.

Discard any oil left in pan. Pour wine or stock carefully around fish. Boil fast for a couple of minutes without disturbing fish. Remove from heat and place crisp vegetables on top of fish. Warm through gently, garnish with parsley and paprika.

Serve with crusty bread.

Serves 4

Bouillabaisse

Soup

4 large brown onions, sliced

½ cup olive oil

pinch of dried or sprig of fresh thyme

2 cloves garlic, crushed

2 tablespoons plain flour

water

½ bottle Sauternes style wine

6 cups fish stock (recipe page 41)

6 egg yolks, beaten

pinch cayenne pepper or a few drops Tabasco sauce

juice of 1 lemon

60 g (2 oz) Parmesan cheese, grated

Fish

olive oil

gemfish or other thick white fish, boned and cut into portions of choice

juice of 1 lemon

pinch chopped tarragon or fresh or dried basil

pepper, freshly ground

salt, to taste

To make the soup, in a large saucepan, fry onions in olive oil until light brown. Add thyme, garlic and flour mixed to a paste with water and stir on low heat for a few minutes. Add the wine and fish stock and simmer for ½ hour. Strain through a fine cloth or strainer.

Pour the strained soup into a clean pan and, just before you are ready to serve, heat through and add the egg yolks, cayenne pepper or Tabasco sauce, lemon juice and Parmesan cheese. Do not boil. Pour over cooked fish fillets and serve.

To cook fish, heat a little olive oil in a pan, add fish, lemon juice and other ingredients and lightly fry until cooked. This should take only a few minutes if the fillets aren't too thick. Place fish carefully in a deep tureen and pour the bouillabaisse soup over them.

Serve with big chunks of crusty bread or bruschetta.

Serves 6

Gemfish is good in this recipe because, in season, it is economical. It is practically boneless and makes nice thick fillets. This bouillabaisse can also be made with other fish.

Crunchy Fish Chowder

I use gemfish for this dish because it is thick and easy to bone. Chowders are generally a mixture of fish varieties, so if you have access to prawns, crayfish or crabs, by all means add them to this dish to make it taste even better!

3 sticks celery, chopped

1 brown onion, chopped

1 small capsicum or ½ large, chopped

2 tablespoons butter

1 teaspoon sugar

3 drops Tabasco sauce

½ teaspoon dried dill

½ teaspoon dried basil

1 bay leaf, whole

pinch nutmeg

1 teaspoon salt

5 cups fish stock (recipe page 41)

1 kg (2 lb) or more thick fish fillets, boned and skinned, either finely chopped or cut into bite-sized pieces

2 cups breadcrumbs, toasted in oven

grated cheese

butter

Place celery, onion and capsicum in a large, heavy pan and fry slowly in butter until soft, stirring all the time. Add sugar and Tabasco sauce and the other seasonings. Stir all these ingredients together. Cook for a few minutes.

Add fish stock, mix all ingredients and cook for 5 minutes. Add the fish. Cook slowly 5 or 6 minutes. If you think there is too much stock in the mixture before you put the fish in, reduce the excess by fast boiling and then add the fish.

Turn all into a flat, shallow ovenproof dish and put breadcrumbs on top. Sprinkle with cheese, dot with butter and place under a hot grill to brown.

Serve with hot garlic bread and creamy buttered potatoes, with a sprinkling of salad herbs.

Serves 3-4

If there is oil floating on top of the chowder when made, that is okay. The toasted breadcrumbs absorb excess oil and the oil flavours the crumbs.

Micky Drip's Seafood Chowder

Served in winter at Fisherman's Wharf, Watsons Bay, this is Michael's speciality. Please order in advance if coming to eat at our place. Probably now that you know how to do it, we have lost a customer. Never mind, you will come back for something else in the seafood line, or just to gaze and dream a little, looking at Sydney Harbour.

Stock

2 fish heads or bones

1½ teaspoons salt

2 bay leaves

1 lemon, sliced

water

Chowder

1 large brown onion, chopped

1 or 2 sticks celery, chopped

1 cup potatoes, diced

2 large tomatoes, peeled and chopped

2 teaspoons curry powder

2 cups milk

1 cup cream

1 kg (2 lb) fillets fresh fish, boned and chopped into pieces

125 g (4 oz) scallops

375 g (13 oz) green (raw) prawns, shelled and de-veined

1 small green mud crab or 2 large raw blue swimmer crabs, cut up

white pepper

dash Tabasco sauce

1 dozen oysters (if feeling lavish)

parsley or celery tops, chopped

Make stock by putting fish heads or bones, salt, bay leaves and lemon into a large saucepan. Cover with water and bring to a boil. Simmer for 30 minutes. Strain bones, cool; remove any fish flesh from bones or head of fish, being careful you do not leave scales behind. Discard bones. Put flesh aside for use in other dishes.

Return stock to clean pot and add onion, celery, potatoes, tomatoes. Add curry powder mixed with milk and cream. Stir in and cook a further 15 minutes. Add fish, scallops, prawns and crab and stir through. Season with pepper and Tabasco sauce. Just before ready to serve, drop oysters in to warm through. Garnish with parsley or celery tops.

Serve with fried bread croutons. People will do the Oliver Twist act for this one, and I reckon you will have to make more. It's very moreish.

Serves 8

Starters, Nibblies & Dips

Some of the best food you can provide when entertaining is made with seafood — delicious dishes you can prepare beforehand and then serve hot or cold. If it is to be a lavish buffet party, some of the recipes can be taken from different sections of this book and cut down to size; this depends on the host or hostess. For parties, I think it is best to keep your food easy to handle. Dry mixtures are preferable, so as to protect valuable furnishings, because buffets are mostly stand-up affairs and food does get spilt.

All the nibblies in this section can be eaten with the fingers or with utensils — ideal party foods. They are delicious served with drinks before smaller dinner parties, too. You can make them instead of a sit-down first course or, if you're feeling lavish, as well!

But, of course, there's no need for an excuse to spoil yourself with some tasty and nutritious treats. Seafood every day of the week? Why not?

Don't be shy of using tinned fish on occasions. And, of course, just because a couple of my recipes use tinned fish, it doesn't mean that you can't substitute fresh cooked fish, or leftovers.

Prawns

To me, prawns always look best unpeeled; that beautiful, red, shining shell is most attractive. (You can always rub them with oil to make them look even better if you have the time.) But, alas, you are not having a prawn night, so you will have to peel them, I'm afraid. If you are like me and just love prawns, get somebody else to do the peeling. Otherwise, the temptation may be so overpowering that you will have to cross prawns off the menu! Shell the prawns, leaving the tails on to hold them by. Make sure the prawns are de-veined and cleaned properly. Arrange them on platters around bowls containing dips or sauces, close together and all facing the one way, with parsley galore. Have fingerbowls and serviettes nearby.

Another way with whole prawns is to spread a cracker biscuit with mayonnaise, top with a prawn, then glaze with gelatine (see recipe for seafood glaze on page 64).

You will find other prawn recipes on pages 107–114.

Our Great Australian Rock Oyster

If you want to be lavish at your cocktail party, place oysters on plates with accompaniments. Oysters go well with lime and lemon wedges, chopped coriander, chopped dill, freshly ground black pepper, wasabi mayonnaise and sweet chilli. Opened oysters dry out quickly, so they are a 'dicey' item for a cocktail party. Don't leave them uncovered, either in or out of the fridge. Cover them with damp greaseproof paper if they have to stand any length of time, and keep cool in the refrigerator. I suggest you serve lots of thinly sliced brown or rye bread with your oysters – they'll go further that way. I hope you know, too, that oysters can vary in size and taste, depending on the season.

Finely cracked ice is good as a bed for oysters, but a nuisance at parties.

If you would like to serve oysters cooked, I've included some popular recipes in this section. There are other oyster recipes in the Seafood section (see pages 126–129).

Seafood Eggs

500 g (1 lb) cooked lobster meat
   (fresh or frozen), chopped very finely, or
   500 g (1 lb) cooked peeled prawns (fresh or frozen),
   chopped

¾ cup mayonnaise

½ teaspoon chilli sauce

1 teaspoon finely chopped red capsicum

1 teaspoon finely chopped green onion (scallions)

a little Tabasco sauce

pinch salt

16 hard-boiled eggs

1 tablespoon chopped parsley

thinly sliced red capsicum

Don't discard those unused egg yolks — they'll make a beautiful dressing for your other dishes (see leghorn sauce, recipe page 148).

Defrost lobster or prawns if frozen.

Combine lobster meat, mayonnaise, chilli sauce, capsicum, onion, Tabasco sauce and salt.

Cut eggs in half lengthwise and remove yolks. Remove a small slice from the outside of the whites so they sit flat on your serving platter. Fill each egg white with spoonfuls of the lobster mixture. Sprinkle with chopped parsley and chill.

Just before serving, place a strip of red capsicum across each egg – remember, eye appeal does the trick every time.

Makes 32

Sashimi

The most important thing with this recipe is to use the freshest best quality ingredients.

150 g (5 oz) fresh tuna

150 g (5 oz) fresh kingfish

150 g (5 oz) fresh ocean trout

150 g (5 oz) grated white radish

wasabi paste or powder

soy sauce

Cut tuna into a rectangular block about 5 cm by 20 cm (2 in by 8 in) and 2 cm (¾ in) thick. Then slice sideways into 1 cm (½ in) wide strips. Cut kingfish and ocean trout in the same way.

Arrange fish slices artistically on a serving plate. Add grated white radish, and place a small amount of wasabi on side of plate. (If using wasabi powder, mix with a little water.) Serve soy sauce in individual small bowls.

Mix a small amount of wasabi with some soy sauce and dip fish into this before eating.

Serves 4

George Heydon's Cold Fish Puffs

Thanks to my old friend and one-time hotel chef, George Heydon, for this recipe.

1 kg (2 lb) boned fish fillets, steamed
salt and pepper
750 g (1½ lb) potatoes, boiled and mashed
2 tablespoons plain flour
1 egg
oil for frying
lemon wedges
tartare sauce (recipe page 147)

Flake the fish and season with salt and pepper to taste. Put aside.

Put the mashed potato in a bowl, add the flour and as much egg as necessary to make a smooth dough.

Place the potato mixture onto a floured board, pat out (with floured hands) to a thickness of about 1 cm (½ in). Cut into 8 cm (3 in) rounds, spoon a little of the fish on each round and gently pat down. Fold over and press the edges together.

Heat the oil in a pan and gently fry the puffs on both sides until golden brown.

Drain, allow to cool, and then chill in the refrigerator. Serve with lemon wedges and tartare sauce.

Makes about 25–30

Creams of the Sea

thinly sliced bread (white, wholemeal or rye)
cream cheese or cheese spread
smoked salmon, salmon, caviar, sardines,
    pickled herring, chopped lobster, crab or prawns
red and green capsicum, finely chopped
stuffed olives
parsley, finely chopped

Cut fancy shapes (stars, diamonds, circles, and so on) from thinly sliced bread. Spread with cream cheese or cheese spread and top with any of the suggested toppings. Garnish with additional cream cheese and finish with a little chopped capsicum, stuffed olives or parsley. This is a little extra trouble, but the finished product is definitely worth it if you are entertaining.

Cucumber and Finely Flaked Fish Sandwiches

cucumber, finely sliced
salt and pepper
cold cooked flaked fish
white onion, grated
rye bread, buttered
lettuce leaves
parsley

Sprinkle the sliced cucumber with salt, leave to drain. Rinse the cucumber and pat dry. Season with a little pepper.

Mix fish and onion.

Place cucumber slices on buttered rye bread, cover with fish mixture, and top with lettuce before closing sandwich. Trim sandwich and shape to please.

Garnish with parsley.

Angels on Horseback

30 oysters on the shell or bottled

pinch dried basil

1 tablespoon finely chopped parsley

½ teaspoon salt

pepper

paprika

10 rashers bacon, rind and fat removed, cut into thirds

Remove oysters from shells, or drain bottled ones. Place them on a dish and coat them with basil, parsley, salt, pepper and a sprinkling of paprika.

Wrap a bacon piece around each oyster, secure with a toothpick and place oysters on the griller. Grill gently for about 8 to 10 minutes (if you have an adjustable griller, keep oysters about 10 cm (4 inches) from heat) until bacon is crisp but not dried up – remember, you have an oyster wrapped up in there and only the bacon needs cooking. Turn carefully and grill the other side in the same way.

Arrange on hot dishes, and garnish attractively.

Makes 30

Oyster Patties

Oysters are delicious luxury morsels of food, so take care not to ruin them by overcooking — they only need warming.

Foundation White Sauce (recipe page 149)

Worcestershire sauce

anchovy sauce (optional)

30 oysters

30 pastry cases (see recipe for creamy fish tartlets, page 53, or buy ready-made ones)

Make the white sauce, add Worcestershire sauce to taste and a dash of anchovy sauce if desired. Add oysters.

Spoon filling into cases, each case containing one oyster. Then warm in a moderate oven for 10 minutes.

Arrange attractively on serving dish.

Makes 30

Fish Cocktail Pieces

3 cups plain flour

salt and pepper

dash Tabasco sauce

4 cups (or more) water

oil for deep-frying

1.5 kg (3 lb) fillets of any thick type of fish,
    such as gemfish, jewfish or kingfish, cut into chunks

parsley

lemon wedges

tartare sauce (recipe page 147)

To make batter, place flour, salt, pepper and Tabasco sauce into a fairly large basin. Add water. With a hand-held beater, beat water into flour until the mixture is thick and creamy. If mixture is too thick, gradually add more water to make it similar to the consistency of pancake batter – plenty of beating does the trick. This is a simple batter, but I find it is the best.

Place sufficient oil to practically cover the fish pieces into a large, deep pan. (Please note that the oil must not have been used before if you want this recipe to be a success.) Heat oil until practically boiling. (I have never seen that blue flame they say appears when it is time to start frying – do your own test by dropping a little batter in the hot oil and, when it rises fast to the top, you will know it is ready.)

I tend to make my fish pieces a little larger than most people do, otherwise they seem to be all batter. Lightly dust each portion with flour, then dip in batter and drop carefully into the hot oil.

Cook for about 10 minutes. Do not overcook – fish is delicate and cooks very quickly – and remember that unless you serve the fish cocktails immediately you will have to reheat them.

When cooked, drain well. Please do not put one on top of another after all your hard work – they will become soggy.

If you need to reheat the fish, make sure the oven is very hot (260°C/500°F), then lower the temperature to about 150°C (300°F) when fish pieces are put in. Please do not dry out these tasty morsels of fish – 10 minutes in the oven is plenty.

Spread sheets of greaseproof paper on your serving dishes and arrange fish pieces on these. Garnish with lots of parsley and lemon wedges and serve with small bowls of tartare sauce.

Makes 20

Lobster Bites

250 g (8 oz) cooked lobster meat, fresh or frozen

24 fresh mushrooms, about 4 cm (1½ in) in diameter

¼ cup condensed cream of mushroom soup

2 tablespoons fine, soft breadcrumbs

2 tablespoons mayonnaise

¼ teaspoon Worcestershire sauce

few drops Tabasco sauce

pepper

grated Parmesan cheese

Preheat oven to 220°C (425°F).

If your lobster is frozen, let it thaw naturally (don't stand it in warm water or run water onto it), and make sure that all particles of shell have been removed. Chop the lobster meat.

Wipe mushrooms with a damp cloth and remove stems. Combine soup, lobster, breadcrumbs, mayonnaise, Worcestershire sauce, Tabasco sauce and pepper to taste. Mix together well. Fill each mushroom cap with a tablespoon of the lobster mixture, sprinkle with cheese and place on a well-greased baking sheet.

Bake in a hot oven for 10 to 15 minutes, or until lightly browned. Decorate with your usual flair.

Makes 24

Roe Titbits

4 large fresh soft fish roes (flathead roes are good)

8 thin strips bacon

lemon juice

butter for frying

8 pieces of bruschetta or buttered
    toast (preferably rye) with crusts removed

anchovy paste or anchovy fillets mashed with a fork

pickled gherkin, cut in strips

freshly ground black pepper

Cut the roes in half lengthwise. Fold each half in two, wrap a strip of bacon around them. Sprinkle with lemon juice and secure with small skewers, string or toothpicks.

Fry gently in hot butter or bake in a hot oven till crisp. In the meantime, spread the bruschetta or toast with anchovy paste and add a few strips of gherkin, cover with buttered greaseproof paper and heat in the oven.

When roes are cooked, remove the skewers and sprinkle with freshly ground pepper. Place roes on bruschetta or toast and serve piping hot.

Serves 5 to 6

Crunchy Celery Fishwich

2 sticks crisp celery, strings
    removed and finely chopped

1 tablespoon mayonnaise

sprinkle paprika

pinch dried basil

2 cups cooked, boned, flaked fish
    (blue eye or salmon would be good)

salt and pepper

small French loaf, sliced horizontally and buttered

Combine celery, mayonnaise, paprika, basil, fish and salt and pepper in blender, or beat together in a basin until well mixed. Spread mixture on bread halves and join together. Can be warmed in oven before serving.

Crumbed Roes

Flathead roes are tender, smooth and flavoursome. I like to prepare them very simply.

flathead or mullet roes

1 egg, beaten

breadcrumbs

butter

lemon wedges

Place roes in a saucepan of warm water, bring to boil and simmer 5 minutes for flathead roes, 15 minutes for mullet roes. Drain and leave to cool. Brush with egg, roll in breadcrumbs and fry in butter until nicely browned. Serve warm with lemon wedges and toast.

Allow 1 flathead roe or ½ large mullet roe per person

Creamy Fish Tartlets

*This scrumptious mixture can be used for so many dishes.
You can buy ready-made patty cases for these tartlets or you
can make your own.*

Pastry

1 cup self-raising flour

1 cup plain flour

pinch salt

170 g (6 oz) clarified butter (see page 149) or
    margarine

1 egg

1 cup water

Filling

1 kg (2 lb) flaked and boned fish
    (gemfish, jewfish, snapper, whitebait,
    canned salmon or whatever you have on hand)

salt and freshly ground pepper

1 teaspoon anchovy essence,
    paste of fillets mashed with a fork

2 large sticks celery, strings removed, finely chopped

1 large carrot, finely grated

1 tablespoon chopped parsley

pinch dried basil

1 tablespoon snipped chives

1 bay leaf, crushed

dash Tabasco sauce

1 onion, finely chopped (optional)

½ cup milk

½ cup water

2 tablespoons plain flour, blended with a little milk

paprika

parsley

To make pastry, sift together self-raising flour, plain flour
and salt. Rub shortening into flour until it resembles fine
breadcrumbs. Beat egg and water together, add to flour
and mix well.

Turn out onto a floured board and, using your floured
rolling pin (or a bottle, if you cannot find the pin), roll out
thinly. If the dough is too hard to roll, put back into bowl,
add a little more water and try again. Cut out rounds and
press lightly into patty tins.

To make filling, mix together fish, salt, pepper, anchovy
essence or paste, celery, carrot, chopped parsley, basil,
chives, bay leaf, Tabasco sauce and onion, if using. Put
mixture into a saucepan with sufficient milk and water
to almost cover the mixture – enough to make it fairly
moist. Boil slowly for about 10 minutes and thicken with
blended flour. Cook for a further 10 minutes, stirring
constantly – please be careful that it does not burn.

Allow the mixture to cool a little. Fill the pastry-lined patty
tins and bake in a hot oven for about 20 minutes. Turn
the tartlets out, arrange on a serving dish and garnish
each one with a sprinkling of paprika and parsley sprigs.

Serve with other hot savouries, or make a feature dish of
them.

Makes 18

*If using whitebait or
canned salmon, make your
sauce first, then add fish
and cook for 5 minutes
only. Also, if you do not
want to make pastry, make
your cases with sandwich
bread. Butter patty tins and
one side of bread. Carefully
place bread, buttered side
down, in tins. Trim and
bake. You can then put
the filling in when they are
cooked — and, of course,
you will reheat when ready.*

Fishermen's Yarns

A few fish yarns from the old–time fishermen of Watsons Bay, just to get that party started:

Mick the Fibber, the laughing cavalier and fisherman, asked Billy Love (one of the greatest snapper set-lines fishermen): 'How did you go last night, Bill?'

'Not bad,' said Bill. 'A couple of baskets of fair-size snapper and, would you believe it, a huge big lobster about seven pound in weight.'

Mick said, 'Funny thing, I caught a large lobster too last week when I was set-lining. As well as a good catch of snapper, this twenty-two pound lobster was attached.'

Experienced and truthful, Bill asked, 'How did it eat, Mick?'

Mick the Fibber replied, 'Cripes, mate, haven't reached the lobster yet, still eating the oysters off the back of it. In a coupla days we hope to get to the lobster flesh.'

Headache (a loving nickname) and Brownie were sitting outside the old boatshed at Watsons Bay, talking about where the fish were biting.

Headache said, 'The jewies are on thick outside the Heads, just about the spot where the Dunbar was wrecked. I caught a huge one, and in fact it had a brass lantern in it – still alight.'

'Lies!' said Brownie. 'I don't believe it.'

'Well,' said Headache, 'you take twelve pound off that fourteen-pound snapper you told me you caught inside the Harbour, and I'll blow out the light in the lantern!'

Potato Tops

This recipe was given to me by Joy Lodge, in her early days a dancer of distinction and for many years a well-known figure at St Luke's Hospital, Sydney. Joy worked in the office and at the reception desk. The dish may be prepared beforehand and popped in the oven just before serving.

1 can sardines or 6 king prawns, shelled

juice of 1 lemon or a little water or vinegar

3 gherkins

onion

salt

parsley, finely chopped

2 stalks celery, strings removed and finely chopped

pepper (cayenne if preferred)

6 pastry boats

small quantity mashed potato

Mash sardines with lemon juice (if using prawns, squeeze juice over them). Chop 2 of the gherkins (keep one for garnishing), and add to mixture with onion, salt, parsley, celery and pepper. Place mixture in pastry boats.

Cover with mashed potato, streaked with a fork or left plain. Garnish with thin rounds of remaining gherkin and place on a tray or pavlova plate. Put in a moderate oven or under the griller for slow heating and browning.

Garnish with more parsley.

Serves 6

Tuna Cheesies

30 rounds Melba toast (see recipe below in method)

250 g (8 oz) can tuna, drained

1 cup shredded cheese

¼ cup butter or margarine, softened

2 tablespoons lemon juice

1½ tablespoons grated onion

1 teaspoon Worcestershire sauce

½ teaspoon paprika

3 drops Tabasco sauce

Make Melba toast first – this is simply thinly sliced bread baked in a hot oven till crisp.

Flake the tuna. Cream the cheese and butter. Add remaining ingredients and tuna. Mix thoroughly. Spread each Melba toast round with approximately 2 teaspoons of tuna mixture.

Place on a baking tray, and grill about 10 cm (4 in) from source of heat for 3 to 5 minutes or until browned.

Makes about 30

Crab Grabs

250 g (8 oz) can crabmeat

shortcrust pastry rounds,
    biscuit thin, or cracker biscuits

½ cup shredded cheese

2 tablespoons mayonnaise

1½ teaspoons chopped chives

few drops of Tabasco sauce

freshly ground pepper

¼ teaspoon salt

2 egg whites

Preheat oven to 180°C (350°F).

Chop crabmeat and put aside. Place pastry rounds (or crackers) on a greased baking slide for about 15 minutes (10 minutes). Cook until light brown, remove from oven and turn over.

Increase oven temperature to 230°C (450°F).

Blend cheese, mayonnaise, chives, Tabasco sauce, pepper and crabmeat. Mix thoroughly.

Add salt to egg whites, beat until stiff but not dry. Fold crab mixture into egg white. Top each biscuit with 1 tablespoon of crab mixture. Bake in a very hot oven for 8 to 10 minutes or until lightly browned.

Makes 20

Tuna Puffs

Puff Shells

½ cup boiling water

¼ cup butter or margarine

pinch salt

½ cup plain flour

2 eggs

Tuna Filling

500 g (1 lb) canned tuna

1 cup celery, strings removed, finely chopped

½ cup mayonnaise

2 tablespoons chopped onion

2 tablespoons sweet pickles, chopped

salt to taste

Preheat oven to 230°C (450°F).

Combine water, butter and salt in a saucepan and bring to boil. Add flour all at once and stir vigorously until mixture forms a ball and leaves the sides of the pan.

Remove from heat. Cool for a while, then add eggs, one at a time, beating thoroughly after each addition. Continue beating until a stiff dough is formed. (If you are making puffs for the first time – and there always has to be a first time – use your saucepan to do all this, especially if you are making only a small amount. You will become such an addict of puff making that you will be making chocolate eclairs and cream puffs in no time.)

When the mixture is smooth and thick, drop level teaspoonfuls onto a well-greased baking sheet, and bake in a very hot oven for 10 minutes. Reduce heat to 175°C (350°F) and continue baking for about 5 to 10 minutes longer. Cool.

To make filling, drain and flake tuna. Combine all ingredients and mix thoroughly. Cut tops from puff shells and fill each shell with about 2 teaspoons of mixture. Serve cold.

Makes about 40

Sardine Dip

2 x 125 g (4 oz) cans sardines

500 g (16 oz) cream cheese, softened

1 tablespoon grated horseradish

2 drops Tabasco sauce

3 tablespoons lemon juice

2 tablespoons grated onion

½ cup crushed potato crisps

2 tablespoons chopped parsley

Drain sardines and mash. Stir the cream cheese, add horseradish, Tabasco sauce, lemon juice, onion and sardines and mix thoroughly. Shape into a mound on a serving plate. Combine potato crisps and parsley and cover sardine mixture completely. Chill.

Serve with breads, crackers or mixed raw vegetables.

Makes about 3 cups

George's Taramasalata

This delicious first course is courtesy of George Andronicus. It is a favourite Greek dish.

1 can tarama (fish roe) (100 g/3½ oz)

1 egg yolk

4 slices stale white bread, soaked in water and squeezed out

1 clove garlic, crushed

½ small onion, finely grated

3-4 tablespoons lemon juice

½ cup olive oil

bread or raw vegetables, cut in strips

Put tarama and egg yolk in blender, mix at low speed and add bread, garlic and onion and blend. When well blended, add lemon juice and olive oil and blend again. Chill.

Serve on a platter with crusty bread or crisp vegetables such as celery, carrot, cauliflower, zucchini.

Marika's Taramasalata

This taramasalata recipe was given to me by Marika Harris, a Greek lady with a grown-up family — and in my opinion a great cook.

1 can tarama (100 g/3½ oz) or other salted fish roe

2 medium potatoes, boiled

1 cup olive oil

juice of 2 lemons

1 onion, greated

chives, finely chopped

crackers

black olives

Using a mortar and pestle, pound fish roe and potatoes to make a fine paste or use a blender and blends to a fine paste. Still using the pestle, add alternate small amounts of oil and lemon juice until all is used. The mixture should be creamy, smooth and thick.

When ready to use, add onion and chives. Spread on cracker biscuits and decorate with halved black olives for delicious canapés.

Fish

Fish

The first recipes in this section are the basics: fish that is deep-fried, pan-fried, grilled, baked, steamed and poached. The techniques are those used in our restaurants. If you like, you could always just serve your fish with lemon butter and parsley, or use one of the sauces in the Dressings, Sauces & Stuffings section (see pages 142–153) for variety.

Customers sometimes say: 'We cook fish at home but cannot get it to taste the same as when we have it at the restaurant. Why?'

Naturally, we buy large fish for the restaurants and fillet them in fairly thick portions ready for frying or grilling. This also means the bones are easier to take out. With your small family, you do not need fish of this proportion, and you buy small fillets of fish, and generally just flour it, put a little oil in the pan and possibly fry it on too fierce a heat. Because fish is so delicate, it needs only a few minutes in the oil, and when it is not covered it tends to dry out even more quickly. You get disappointed with your small fillets of fish and start to get frustrated at having to pick bones out of your mouth.

Techniques for Cooking Fish

Spend a little extra time selecting fish, and if you happen to have bones in the fish you have, take out as many as you can first. This goes for grilling, too. And remember the number one rule – the fresher the fish, the better the dish.

The following hints will also help:

Handle your fish with tender loving care. Don't fry or grill it with gay abandon – stay at your stove so you can regulate the heat and therefore have a perfect result. Delicate seafood cooks very quickly.

Remember that small fish or fillets with a lot of bone are best pan-fried, steamed or grilled and served simply, without thick sauces. Fillets or steaks of large fish, such as jewfish, snapper and barramundi, are good for dishes that contain a lot of sauce and, if fried or grilled, should always be served with a sauce as they tend to be dry.

Before cooking, check that the fish is perfectly cleaned, and remove any odd scales that might have been overlooked. Remove as many bones as you can.

The recipes in this section sometimes specify a particular kind of fish and at other times give a choice or do not specify at all. Remember that you can always substitute one kind of fish for another. Just use a similar type of fish to the one in the recipe. If you're not sure of a substitution in season, ask your friendly fishmonger!

Refer to the Before You Start section of this book (pages 28-37) for information on some of the more common table fish, including their flesh type, availability in different parts of the country, and the names by which they are known in different States/Territories.

Deep-frying Fish

Fried fish and chips for dinner is a good family get-together meal. Bring out your large serving plates for fish and use vegetable dishes to hold the hot chips. Put out plates of cut-up lemons, bread or rolls already buttered, tartare sauce (recipe page 147) and cocktail sauce (recipe page 147), even Worcestershire sauce (lots of people like this) and vinegar, plus salad, of course. Hot plates are essential. Everybody sits down together and serves themselves from the centre plates piled high with fish and chips.

Cool watermelon, rockmelon (cantaloupe), honeydew, paw-paw or whatever fruits are in season make the perfect dessert after a meal of fish and chips.

The secret of deep-frying is to use plenty of fresh oil. All oil (if any is left) should be discarded after frying fish because of the sediment remaining in the pan. The type of oil to use is a matter of choice. Olive oil is perfect as the fish will still be tasty and enjoyable when cold. I think it is the only oil that keeps the fish like this. You can also use one of the polyunsaturated oils, such as safflower or sunflower oil, for deep-frying.

When deep-frying or pan-frying, you should never leave your pan with the heat full on. If you are called away, remove it from the stove and, at all times, have handy a heavy lid that fits over the pan or saucepan. If you have a fire, do not run outside with the pan, but put the lid on immediately to smother the flame, then turn the heat off.

Use a deep heavy-gauge saucepan – one that you make your jam in or use to cook the winter steamed pudding. Half-fill your pan with whatever oil you prefer. Heat the oil until very hot but not boiling. Some people say to look for a blue flame that comes from the oil in the pan and put the fish in when it appears. I can honestly say that in all the years I have been cooking fish and observed it cooking in the large deep-fryers, I have never seen that flame. I certainly have the oil very, very hot when I carefully place the fish in, but not boiling. If the oil was boiling the fish would be ruined – cooked on the outside immediately and raw inside – especially thick fish.

Coat your fish with a good batter (see recipes on this page). Using your tongs, fingers or a spatula, place battered fillets of fish in very hot oil and cook for 5 to 10 minutes, depending on the size, until golden brown. Do not try to cook too many fillets at once.

Remove fillets from pan. Drain and, if necessary, place on a serving plate in the oven at a very low heat to keep warm while you cook the rest of the fish. Do not pile the cooked fillets on top of one another or they will become soggy.

There are many different recipes for making batter for coating fish, croquettes, fish cakes, shellfish, and so on. Once you find the one you like, I suggest you stick with it, as we have. Anyway, as requested so often and repeated so many times to people from all parts of the world, here is the Doyles batter recipe. It is dead simple. The 'secret' is in the beating.

It takes time to make the perfect batter, but you know the old saying: 'If it's worth doing, it's worth doing well.'

Doyles Deep-frying Batter

½ cup to 1 cup plain flour

1 cup cold water, plus 1 extra cup

Place the flour in a basin. Add the 1 cup of water then, with a rotary hand-held beater, start beating. Gradually add your extra cup of water and beat until you get plenty of 'body' into that batter. You may have to add more water. The result has to be a thin, smooth, well-bodied batter that adheres to a wooden spoon.

Keep testing by dipping the spoon in and letting the batter drop slowly back into the mixture. If it drops slowly it's okay and ready to use.

Our only other 'secrets' are plenty of beautiful, fresh clean oil and the fish to go with it.

Another Frying Batter

125 g (4 oz) plain flour

½ teaspoon salt

½ cup tepid water

1 tablespoon vegetable oil or clarified butter (see page 149)

two egg whites, stiffly whisked

Put flour and salt into a basin. Gradually add water and vegetable oil or clarified butter. Mix into a smooth batter. If time permits, put batter aside for about 1 hour. Just before using, lightly stir in egg whites.

Tim's Beer Batter

Even after all my years of battering fish, Tim, our youngest son tells me: 'Mum, I think I have worked out the best batter of all.'

375 ml (12 fl oz) light beer

2 egg whites, beaten until soft peaks form

1 soup spoon olive oil

pinch salt and pepper

2 cups best-quality plain flour

Mix all ingredients together, adding flour last. Using a hand-held beater or whisk, beat until smooth. (If you like a fluffier batter, the beaten egg whites can be folded in last thing.)

Coat fish lightly in plain flour, and dip into batter. Fish pieces should not be too large, and don't overload your deep-fryer with cooking oil.

Fry fish in very hot oil (not less than 185°/375°F) for 5 to 10 minutes, according to thickness of fish.

Poaching Fish

Place fish fillets or steaks in a pan with just enough water to cover. Add a little chopped onion and celery, a few peppercorns, a bay leaf, a pinch of dried basil and about 1 tablespoon tarragon vinegar or brown vinegar.

Cover with lid, bring to the boil, reduce heat to low and simmer slowly for 10 or 15 minutes, depending on thickness of fish. Test with a fork to see if fish is cooked; if it flakes easily, it is done.

Remove fish from liquid with a spatula and place on hot plates. Reserve stock to make a sauce (see below).

Sauce for Poached Fish

Melt 1 tablespoon butter in a clean saucepan and add 3 tablespoons of plain flour, mixing together. Gradually add strained stock in which fish was cooked. Stir over heat until smooth and thickened.

Pour sauce over poached fish, garnish with parsley and lemon wedges.

Steaming Fish

This method of cooking fish is perfect for people on low-fat diets.

If you have a steamer, fill it with about 8 cm (3 in) or more (according to size of steamer) of water and bring to the boil. Season fish with salt and pepper and wrap in foil or baking paper.

Place fish in steamer and steam for about 10 minutes or more, according to size of fish.

If you don't have a steamer, just put the seasoned fish on a buttered plate with another plate over it, or cover with foil, and steam over a saucepan.

Serve steamed fish with butter and parsley sauce (foundation white sauce with finely chopped parsley – recipe page 149).

Pan-frying Fish

Pan-frying is often the best cooking method when you have small fillets of fine-textured fish, such as whiting, John Dory or silver bream. For something extra special, may I suggest you fry in pure olive oil. You can then enjoy your fish hot or cold, served with freshly ground pepper and salt and lashings of lemon.

Then, of course, it is also delicious fried in butter or your favourite frying oil. I think margarine, especially polyunsaturated, tends to stick to the pan.

To Pan-fry 6 Large Fillets

Beat 2 eggs in 1 cup of milk and put aside. Dip each fillet into plain flour seasoned with salt and pepper. Shake off excess. Dip floured fillets into egg mixture and place in a pan containing a little oil that has been heated almost to boiling point. (Alternatively, you can roll fillets in breadcrumbs – see below – as a final step before placing in the pan.) Cook until golden – about 10 minutes if the fillets are thin, 15 minutes if thick. Please don't overcook.

Serve with lemon wedges dipped in finely chopped parsley.

Breadcrumbs for Pan-fried Fish and Seafood

Place slices of bread in a hot oven and bake until dry and crisp. Remove from oven and crush with a rolling pin or process them in a blender. (I think it's quicker to crush.) After the dry bread is crushed, store in an airtight jar or tin.

Grilling Fish

You can just imagine what it must be like grilling fish in a restaurant as busy as ours. It takes a lot of care to grill the fish to a turn so that it doesn't dry out. There are certain kinds of fish we don't like to grill; flathead, for example, tends to dry out too much — at least I think so. Our method is as follows.

Place the fish in a shallow pan with a little water and butter. For whole fish, make two shallow cuts on each side.

Brush the fish with melted butter, pop it under a hot griller, reduce the heat slightly, and baste again with melted butter as it cooks. Cooking time depends on the thickness of the fish – 10 to 15 minutes for thick fillets, but for whole fish, 8 to 10 minutes each side.

When it is done, place the fish on a hot serving plate and pour over some hot butter and chopped parsley. Serve a nice sauce with your grilled fish (see the Dressings, Sauces & Stuffings section) to correct any dryness.

Add extra milk to the egg mixture to make it go further.

When I fry oysters, I like to use crushed Sao biscuit crumbs instead of breadcrumbs, and of course you can always buy breadcrumbs or use substitutes like wheatgerm or bran. But I think homemade breadcrumbs give the best result.

Smoking Fish

I must give my thanks for this recipe to my pal from our young days, the late Ray Thomas, one of a family of six sons born in Watsons Bay.

How to Make a Smokebox

Take two standard tea-chests, remove the end of one and both ends of the other. Stand the one with the end on top of the one without ends, making the attached end the top of the box. Then fasten chests together, using the removed ends to 'patch' the joins. Then open one side of both chests to make the door to the smokebox.

In the side of the box, starting about 5 cm (about 2 in) from the top, drill eight holes of 3 mm (about ⅛ in) diameter, placing them 5 cm (about 2 in) apart. Do this to both sides of the box, with 30 cm (about 12 in) between rows of holes. Make wire skewers (No. 8 wire preferably) 45 cm (about 18 in) long to fit across the inside of the box. Stand the box on a flat surface.

There are several kinds of fish that smoke well, but tailor, mullet and luderick (blackfish) are about the best to smoke.

fish, gutted, washed and cleaned, minus backbone and
    head (you can ask your fishmonger to do this for you)

1 kg (2 lb) cooking salt

½ kg (1 lb) brown sugar

water

clean sawdust (see note below)

Split the fish down the back. Mix salt and sugar well. Rub this mixture into the flesh of fish, then place fish in a clean container. (A plastic dustbin makes a good container.)

Add enough fresh water to cover fish and let stand for 1½ hours. Remove from brine, hang fish in the smokebox and let drip-dry.

When the fish feel sticky to touch, they are ready for smoking.

Place sawdust in bottom of the smokebox and light. Keep smoke on fish for 9 hours, then remove from box.

Keep your smoked fish in a cool place for future use.

NOTE: Ensure the sawdust is clean and is safe to use with food. Some timbers are unsuitable. Some eucalypts give a turpentine flavour so check before using. The wood from fruit trees – apples, almonds, apricot – impart a lovely flavour. Hickory is also popular.

Opposite: Early Sunday morning, looking out onto Watsons Bay from Doyles on the Beach.

Baking Fish

It's fair to say that the size of the fish to be baked makes the difference between a 'triumph' and a 'might have been'.

Start off with a fish of at least 2 kg (4 lb) – even better, 3 kg (6 lb) or larger.

Preheat oven to hot, about 200°C (400°F). Prepare fish, making sure it is well cleaned and scaled. Leave the head on. You may choose to stuff the fish with your favourite stuffing (see page 153) or just sprinkle pepper and salt inside it.

Grease a baking dish with butter or oil and arrange fish. To make fish 'stand up' as if it was swimming, put a small bowl inside its head.

Season with pepper and salt, rub over with oil using a brush or your fingers, and cover fish loosely with foil or baking paper. Decrease oven heat to moderate (180°C/350°F) and bake fish from 40 minutes for a 2 kg (4 lb) fish to 1½ hours for a larger fish.

When the fish is cooked, remove to a warm serving plate. Serve with parsley and lemon. Alternatively, allow fish to become cold, then glaze (below) and decorate with vegetables.

Place fish in centre of table and carefully carve, first finishing one side and then turning to the other side. It is best if you can cut the fish in squares if it is large. A big serving spoon is a help, to catch the small pieces as they fall. After you have finished, only the fish's frame should be standing there – just like the fish skeleton you see a cat drag along in a cartoon.

Seafood Glaze

Whole baked fish that is glazed and decorated makes an attractive centrepiece on a buffet table. We use the following glaze for our functions and have always found it quite satisfactory. It can be used to glaze starters, too – prawns or sardines on biscuits, for example, look much more attractive shining with glaze.

The food to be glazed should have been previously cooked and allowed to cool. Cold whole fish is just as delicious as hot.

Dissolve 1 teaspoon gelatine in ⅔ cup hot seasoned stock or hot water flavoured with lemon juice and a little sugar to taste. A touch of sherry is a tasty addition, too. Allow to cool. Lightly brush a little solution over the food. For decoration around your large baked fish, have ready well-drained fruit and vegetables, such as capsicum (thinly sliced), carrot flowers and sticks, asparagus spears and so on, and arrange them around the fish and plate. Paint over again with the solution to give a shiny glaze.

Good Old-fashioned Fish Recipes

Here are some great old recipes for fish stews, fish pies, barbecued fish and fish rissoles. They are all favourites of mine, cooked for many years by my grandmother, my mother or my old friends at Watsons Bay and now enjoyed regularly by our family at home. They're hard to beat!

Fish Head Stew

Ask your friendly fishmonger to keep some fish heads for you.

1 large head of any fish (jewfish, cod, snapper
    or kingfish, for example), scaled

salt and pepper

3 tablespoons vinegar

butter

1 onion, chopped

500 g (1 lb) mushrooms, chopped

2 large tomatoes, chopped

2 sticks celery, chopped

1 tablespoon cornflour

1 tablespoon Worcestershire sauce

2 dashes Tabasco sauce

curry powder (optional)

Boil the fish head in sufficient water to cover it. Add salt, pepper and vinegar. After it has come to the boil, simmer slowly for 20 minutes. Be careful not to break its shape.

Melt butter in a pan and fry the vegetables carefully. Keep stirring them so that they do not burn.

Pour half the water off the fish head and add the vegetables. Make a paste of the cornflour with a little water and the Worcestershire and Tabasco sauces. Stir in curry powder, if desired. Add paste to the fish and vegetables and cook gently for 10 minutes or so (depending on the size of the fish head).

Place in a baking dish or large casserole and serve with the head in a 'swimming' position, the vegetables surrounding it.

Serve this dish with fresh chips. You'll need fingers, thumbs and a spoon!

Hannah Newton's Fish Stew

Any day you walk into my home you will find fish in the fridge! Here's Hannah's makeshift meal. Use one, all or some of the seafood I mention.

black or silver bream, cleaned, scaled and washed

leatherjackets, cleaned, skinned and washed

sand flathead, cleaned, scaled and washed

blue swimmer crabs, prepared for cooking
    (see note below)

oil for frying

3 large onions, chopped

1 teaspoon salt

2 kg (4 lb) potatoes, peeled and finely chopped

½ teaspoon dried thyme

Put fish into a large pot, boiler or fish kettle.

Heat oil in a large pan, fry onions, stirring all the time. Add salt. Add potatoes and fill the pan with water. Boil for a few minutes, then pour over the fish. Add more water if necessary to cover all the fish. Add thyme and simmer for about 20 minutes.

Do not overcook the fish, and take care when eating fish with small bones.

Serves 6

NOTE: To prepare the crabs for cooking, slip a knife under the shell at the back of the crab and lift shell from body. Clean out waste under a running tap.

Crack claws with a wooden mallet or small hammer. With a sharp knife, cut crab in half or quarters.

Grandma Newton used to tell us that at times she had to do the best she could for dinner with Grandfather's catch of the day.

Jim Smith's Curried Fish

What a healthy, much-loved character was Jim Smith of Watsons Bay. He lived a long, long life and existed mainly on his own catches of fish. Many a time I've had this, his dish, which he made with whatever he caught that day. Flathead was one of his favourites, as was rock cod.

60 g (2 oz) butter

1 kg (2 lb) flathead (or cod), washed, dried, skinned and boned, and cut into chunks about 4 cm (1½ in) square or 1 kg (2 lb) fish fillets

1 medium brown onion, sliced

2 teaspoons curry powder

1 tablespoon plain flour

2 cups fish stock (recipe page 41)

1 tablespoon lemon juice

cayenne pepper

salt and pepper

Be careful of small bones in the fish.

Melt the butter in a saucepan and fry fish lightly for a few minutes. Remove fish from pan and set aside.

Put onion, curry powder and flour in the pan. Make sure there is enough butter to fry, and cook slowly for 15 minutes. Do not let the onion get too brown.

Add stock, stir until it boils and then simmer for 20 minutes. Add lemon juice and a sprinkle of cayenne pepper. Season with salt and pepper.

Add fish very, very slowly. On a low flame, cook for 30 minutes so that the fish absorbs the curry flavour. Make sure you put a tight-fitting lid over the saucepan. Stir occasionally so the fish does not stick to the bottom and burn.

Serve with some old-fashioned chutney, boiled rice, and lemon wedges.

Serves 4 or 5

Tasty Fish Casserole

1 kg (2 lb) fish fillets

2 brown onions, chopped

butter

1 kg (2 lb) potatoes, parboiled and sliced

1 dried bay leaf, crushed or fresh, chopped

freshly ground pepper

salt

Preheat oven to 220°C (425°F).

Steam fish for 10 minutes in enough water to cover. Retain stock.

Fry onions in butter until tender, but do not burn. Place fillets of cooked fish and sliced potatoes alternately in casserole dish, ending with potatoes on top. Cover with stock from fish, to which bay leaf, pepper and salt have been added.

Place, uncovered, in hot oven. Decrease heat to 180°C (350°F) and cook until contents are heated through (about 20 minutes).

Serves 4 or 5

The Great Australian Fish Pie

This will rival the meat pie! Delicious!

Pastry

300 g (10 oz) butter or margarine

2 cups plain flour

2 cups self-raising flour

½ teaspoon salt

2 eggs

½ cup cold water

extra plain flour for rolling out

Fish for Filling

1.5 kg (3 lb) thick fish, filleted,
    boned, cut up fish bones (optional)

water

1 brown onion, chopped

2 sticks celery, including tops, chopped

4 bay leaves

1 teaspoon dried basil

1 teaspoon dill

1 teaspoon salt

Filling Mixture

2 tablespoons butter

½ cup plain flour

fish stock (recipe page 41)

fish, prepared as directed, flaked

3 sticks celery, strings removed, finely chopped

½ small can anchovies (about 9), chopped

1 teaspoon Worcestershire sauce

Tabasco sauce, to taste

½ teaspoon dried dill

½ teaspoon dried basil

½ teaspoon nutmeg

salt (optional)

parsley

paprika

Anchovies are quite salty, so be careful when adding salt to this dish

Preheat oven to 180°C (350°F).

To make pastry, rub butter or margarine in flour and salt until it resembles fine breadcrumbs. (If you have a blender or a food processor, it's a breeze!)

Beat eggs in the water for a couple of seconds until mixed. Add water and eggs to flour mixture and stir in until you have a nice wet dough. If the dough is too hard, add some more water. You will soon get the feel of it. If you think, 'I will have to put more flour as I roll it out and it will not be so "short"', don't worry. After you have rolled it out you can spread some more margarine or butter over it before you fold up and roll again.

Roll out pastry to fit the tins you are using. Make the pastry thin. Grease tins, place pastry in; prick bottom of pastry and place some greaseproof paper in centre. Put some dried beans or something like that on top of paper to stop pastry from rising in the centre.

Cook in oven until lightly browned. Take out and discard paper and beans.

To prepare the fish for the filling mixture, place fish and, if you have them, the fish bones as well in a large boiler. Cover with water. Add vegetables and the seasonings, including salt.

Bring to the boil and simmer for 15 minutes. When cooked, strain everything through a fine strainer or cloth and reserve stock.

When cool enough to handle, separate fish from vegetables, remove and discard all bones. Put aside until ready for use in filling mixture.

For the filling mixture, place butter in saucepan and melt. Add flour and, with a wooden spoon, stir until all flour is absorbed. Slowly stir in the stock and gradually add more stock to obtain a thick consistency. You will not use all the stock; put it aside for use in other recipes.

Add flaked fish, celery, anchovies, the sauces, dill, basil, nutmeg and salt, if using. Cook for only 5 minutes. If you think the mixture is a bit thin, make up some white sauce (recipe page 149) and, when cooked, add this to the mixture. Add in parsley.

Place the mixture in the cooked pie shells, sprinkle with paprika.

Alternatively, put a glaze on top of the pie before warming through. Beat two eggs with about 6 tablespoons cream and a pinch of cayenne pepper and brush over each pie. Place back in oven and warm through for about 10 minutes.

Serve piping hot with side vegetables.

Makes 4 pies the size of pizza or pavlova plate. I always make a number and freeze a couple for later use.

Savoury Fish Pie

You'll need a top and a bottom for this pie! See The Great Australian Fish Pie (recipe page 69) for the basic pastry mixture. You may need to adjust pastry amount to suit your pie dish.

You can use this recipe for curried fish pies and all kinds of combinations of seafoods. The main thing to remember is to be sure you have boned the fish well before putting it into the pie shell.

750 g (1½ lb) fish, boned and filleted

salt, to taste

60 g (2 oz) butter

1 brown onion, chopped

garlic (optional)

2 sticks celery, finely chopped

1 capsicum, chopped

4 medium tomatoes or
   1 can tomatoes, drained (reserve juice)

2 bay leaves, crushed or fresh, chopped

½ teaspoon dried basil

½ teaspoon dried dill

1 teaspoon sugar

freshly ground pepper

1 cup white wine or water or juice of canned tomatoes

chopped parsley

pastry for pie case and top (recipe page 69)

milk or cream

Preheat oven to 180°C (350°F).

Poach fish gently in water and salt for 10 minutes.

Melt butter in pan and fry onion without browning. If wanted for flavour, rub a clove of garlic around the pan and then discard.

Add celery, capsicum, tomatoes, bay leaves, basil, dill, sugar, pepper and salt. Fry everything together for 15 minutes. Add wine or other liquids and cook for a further 5 minutes.

Add flaked fish and parsley. Stir and warm through. Turn heat off.

Roll out pastry for top and bottom of pie, as thinly as possible. Line a pie plate with one piece of pastry. Prick bottom of pastry and place some greaseproof paper in centre. Put some dried beans or something similar on top of paper to stop pastry from rising in the centre.

Cook in oven until lightly browned. Take out and discard paper and beans.

Place fish mixture in pie case. Cover with pastry and brush with milk or cream. Reduce oven temperature to 170°C (325°F). Bake until top is brown.

Serve this pie with creamy mashed potatoes.

Serves 3 or 4

Fish and Cheese Pie

See The Great Australian Fish Pie (recipe page 69) for the basic pastry mixture. You may need to adjust pastry amount to suit your pie dish.

500 g (1 lb) fish fillets, steamed and boned

pre-baked pastry shell (recipe page 69)

½ can anchovies (about 9), chopped

2 small, firm tomatoes, sliced

2 sticks celery, finely chopped

½ onion, grated

1 cup foundation white sauce (recipe page 149)

pinch paprika

pinch nutmeg

pinch dried basil

pinch dried dill

2 eggs

½ cup cream

3 drops Tabasco sauce

½ cup grated Parmesan cheese,
   or ¾ cup grated tasty cheddar cheese

parsley, to garnish

Cool fish, place small pieces on the pre-baked pastry shell. Add anchovies and scatter around. Arrange tomatoes, celery and onion over the top.

Into the white sauce mix paprika, nutmeg, basil and dill. Add sauce to the fish in pastry shell, spoon by spoon.

Beat eggs in cream with Tabasco sauce and then gently pour over the mixture in the pie plate. Put pie back into warm oven (170°C/325°F) and cook slowly for 15 minutes.

Remove pie from oven; spread cheese on top and place under a hot grill to brown. Be careful of burning if you are using the Parmesan and not cheddar. Garnish with parsley to serve.

Serves 4

Eva Newton's Fish Pie

Although my mother had no Cordon Bleu diploma, she was a fantastic cook. Mum loved to cook and I do too, but I think she had it over me with lots of dishes. This was one of her masterpieces.

1 kg (2 lb) thick fish (cod, gemfish,
    snapper or jewfish, for example)

1 dozen scallops

6 large green (raw) prawns, peeled and de-veined

1 dozen oysters (fresh or bottled)

1 teaspoon salt

freshly ground pepper

nutmeg

1 bay leaf

pinch dried basil

1 cup melted butter or
    clarified butter (see page 149)

250 g (½ lb) shortcrust pastry or mashed potatoes

grated cheese

cream

paprika

Preheat oven to (170°C/325°F).

Put fish, scallops and prawns in a saucepan and add enough water to just cover. Cook for 8 minutes.

Put oysters in a saucepan, cover with a little water. If fresh, shell and add juice from shells to pan too. Simmer for a few minutes.

Divide the fish into large flakes and place in an ovenproof dish. Lay the oysters on top, season with salt and pepper, nutmeg and other seasonings. Add the melted or clarified butter and cover with shortcrust or with mashed potatoes. Sprinkle cheese on top, wipe over with cream, add a sprinkle of paprika and bake until brown.

Serves 5 to 6

Flathead Pie

1 dozen oysters (bottled or fresh)

750 g (1½ lb) flathead, steamed, boned and cooled

1 cup melted butter or clarified butter (see page 149)

salt

freshly ground pepper

pinch nutmeg

250 g (½ lb) shortcrust pastry or mashed potatoes

Preheat oven to (170°C/325°F).

Simmer oysters for a few minutes in a little water. Divide the fish into large flakes, put half of it into a dish, lay the oysters on top; add melted butter, sprinkle with salt, pepper and nutmeg and cover with the rest of the fish.

Cover dish with pastry or mashed potatoes.

Bake in a warm oven for 30 minutes.

Serve with vegetable sauce (recipe below), or with vegetables and lemon.

Serves 5 or 6

Vegetable Sauce for Flathead Pie

4 medium-sized ripe tomatoes, chopped

2 stalks celery, finely chopped

1 onion, finely chopped

1 teaspoon sugar

½ teaspoon dried basil

1 bay leaf

parsley

lemon wedges

Put the first six ingredients in a saucepan and cook for 10 to 15 minutes.

Serve and sprinkle with parsley and lemon wedges.

The Great Australian Barbecue

Surprise! Surprise! This time not those T-bones, sausages or chops but beautiful, big, fat fish. Blackfish is delicious, mullet has a taste of its own. Barbecue large thick fillets of kingfish, jewfish or any fish. When it's fresh, it's all delicious. Here is the way we used to cook them at our hotel barbecue, which was outside on the lawn.

2 kg (4 lb) fish fillets or whole fish, cleaned

1 large brown onion, sliced

1 capsicum, green or red, sliced

salt

freshly ground pepper

½ cup melted butter

Tabasco sauce

1 large can tomatoes

Use whole, unpeeled potatoes wrapped in foil with this fish. Spread over some sour cream mixed with chives or green onions. Really super!

Place the fish on heavily buttered aluminium foil, supported, if you like, in an old baking dish. Put the onion and capsicum over the fish, and add salt and pepper, butter and Tabasco sauce to taste. Pour the tomatoes carefully over the top.

Cover with more heavily buttered foil and crimp edges to hold in the liquid from the tomatoes. Place over a low charcoal fire; let cook for about 20 minutes. If fish is large, make a small hole in top layer of foil and continue cooking until the fish is tender. Otherwise, serve immediately.

Serves 4

Flo's Old-fashioned Rissoles

The new generation call them hamburgers, fishburgers, fish patties, fish cakes, and so on, but old-fashioned Flo calls them rissoles, and they are very tasty. Here is the recipe.

1 kg (2 lb) thick fish (gemfish, jewfish, kingfish or snapper, for example), boned and scaled

2 stalks celery, strings removed, chopped

1 small brown onion, chopped

½ red capsicum, chopped

grated rind and juice of 1 lemon

2 bay leaves

2 drops Tabasco sauce

parsley

salt and pepper

500 g (1 lb) potatoes, cooked and mashed

plain flour

1 egg

½ cup milk

Sao biscuit crumbs

olive oil for frying

Place fish in saucepan and add enough water to cover. Add celery, onion, capsicum, lemon rind and juice, bay leaves, Tabasco, parsley and salt and pepper. Bring to boil gently and boil uncovered for 10 minutes. Cool.

Add mashed potatoes and mix.

Form into flat rissoles with your hand and roll in plain flour, then dip in egg and milk. Then roll in biscuit crumbs. You can put these rissoles on a dish and leave covered in the fridge overnight if you want to cook them the next day. Fry in hot olive oil for 10 minutes.

Serve with vegetable sauce (recipe page 149).

Makes 14

Opposite: Young Lewis Doyle holding aloft his catch before returning it to the sea

Non-traditional Fish Dishes

Now for some more 'sophisticated' recipes — some of my own favourites and some gathered together 'with a little help from my friends'. I asked some of the Consuls General here in Sydney for their favourite fish recipes and recipes typical of their countries, and also invited some well-known personalities to contribute their most delicious dinner party dishes (fish, of course!). Thanks to their kind responses, this section has everything from Japanese Teriyaki to Jewish Gefillte Fish.

Hope you enjoy these as much as I did when I was testing them!

Tempura of Garfish and Asparagus

Garfish are easily recognised by their lower jaw or 'beak', which is often bright orange or scarlet. These small, slender fish have a delicate, sweet flavour.

Tempura Batter

300 g (2 cups) plain flour, sifted

1 cup ice cubes

3 cups water

Fish and Vegetable

12 medium garfish, butterflied and boned with
    tail intact (ask your fishmonger to do this for you)

plain flour

16 fresh asparagus spears, trimmed and blanched

vegetable oil for deep-frying

To make the batter, whisk the flour and water in a large bowl until almost smooth. Add the cup of ice cubes and stir, then cover and refrigerate for 1 hour.

Dust the garfish and asparagus spears with the flour and shake to remove any excess flour.

Stir the batter and dip the fish and asparagus into the batter, allowing the excess to drip off. Deep-fry the battered fish and asparagus in hot vegetable oil until golden brown. Drain.

Serve with sweet chilli dipping sauce.

Serves 4

Teriyaki

This recipe was kindly supplied by a former Information Officer for the Japanese Consul General in Sydney, Mr H. Date, with the help of his librarian, Miss K. Hyodo. Thank you very much.

2 fillets kingfish or similar fish, 80–100 g (3–3⅓ oz)
    each (I used gemfish, but you could use any large
    fish fillets, such as jewfish, pearl perch or flathead)

1 tablespoon soy sauce

1 tablespoon mirin (substitute sake
    and sugar, or sweet sherry, if necessary)

lemon juice or freshly grated horseradish

Marinate whole fillets in soy sauce and mirin for 1 to 2 hours.

Thread each fillet onto two parallel skewers to keep it firm, and grill until cooked. Serve with lemon juice or freshly grated horseradish.

Serves 2

Shioyaki

Another great recipe from the Japanese Consul General. This is easy to cook and is something a little bit different for a barbecue.

2 small sea bream (morwong)

salt

lemon juice or soy sauce

grated ginger

Clean and scale fish. Rub inside and out with salt and let stand 30 to 40 minutes.

Thread two large skewers through each fish from mouth to tail, prick all over to prevent sputtering, and grill for 10 minutes each side.

Serve with lemon juice or soy sauce, and grated ginger.

Serves 2

The Japanese cook this dish over an open flame — if you can do this, don't let the fish too near the flame, as it burns easily.

Pacific Platter

6-8 large fillets fish

1 tablespoon olive oil

2 tablespoons brown vinegar

1 large clove garlic, crushed

salt and freshly ground pepper

2 bay leaves

1 brown onion, sliced

1 medium can tomatoes, drained (reserve juice)

Sauce

1 brown onion, finely chopped

2 large sticks celery, finely chopped

6 peppercorns

½ teaspoon dried basil, or sprig fresh basil

juice from tinned tomatoes

1 large clove garlic, crushed

Preheat oven to 220°C (425°F).

Place fillets in baking dish, add oil, vinegar, garlic, salt and pepper, bay leaves and sliced onion. Add drained tomatoes to fish fillets. Put baking dish in hot oven, reduce heat to moderate (180°C/350°F) and cook for 15 to 20 minutes.

Simmer sauce ingredients together in a saucepan for 15 minutes. When fish is cooked, arrange on a platter and pour sauce over.

Alternatively, serve fish with curry sauce (recipe page 151) or sweet and sour sauce (recipe page 150), accompanied by bruschetta, or crusty or garlic bread.

Serves 6

Fish with Herbs

This recipe was given to me by Tammie Fraser, wife of Malcolm Fraser, Australia's Prime Minister 1975–1983. It's one of those simple yet elegant dishes.

8 fillets fish, each about 100 g (3 oz)

lemon juice

salt

100 g (3 oz) speck, medium fat, finely chopped

2 onions, finely chopped

500 g (1 lb) tomatoes, peeled, seeded and sliced

1 bunch chives, finely chopped

1 bunch dill, finely chopped

1 bunch parsley, finely chopped

½ bunch cress, finely chopped

½ cup sour cream

½ teaspoon tarragon

salt and freshly ground white pepper

2 tablespoons breadcrumbs

Preheat oven to 180°C (350°F).

Wash and drain the fish, then sprinkle with a little lemon juice and salt.

Place half the speck, onions and sliced tomatoes in an ovenproof dish and lay fish fillets on top.

Add chives, dill, parsley and cress to sour cream with tarragon, salt and pepper. Pour mixture over fish fillets. Cover with remaining speck, onions and tomatoes and sprinkle with breadcrumbs.

Cover dish with foil and bake for 15 minutes.

Serves 4

Oriental Barbecued Bream

This easy-to-make but delectable recipe was kindly supplied by Phil Nadin, former General Manager of the then NSW Fish Marketing Authority. He recommends sea bream as a good budget buy and finds fillets easier to barbecue than whole fish, as you can see how the fish is cooking.

¼ cup polyunsaturated oil

¼ cup soy sauce

2 tablespoons sherry

2 green onions (scallions), sliced

1 clove garlic, crushed

2 teaspoons chopped root ginger

750 g (1½ lb) sea bream fillets

Combine oil, soy sauce, sherry, green onions, garlic and ginger. Mix until well combined.

Add bream fillets and allow to marinate for 1 to 2 hours. Drain; reserve marinade.

Place on a well-greased barbecue plate or grill. Cook for approximately 2 to 3 minutes each side, basting frequently with reserved marinade.

Serves 4 to 6

Mona Mitchell's Fish à la Florentine

4 thick fillets fish

1 cup dry white wine or lemon juice

Topping

1 bunch silverbeet, cooked

1 cup béchamel sauce (recipe page 150)

salt and freshly ground pepper

1 cup brown breadcrumbs

60 g (2 oz) grated cheese

Preheat oven to 170°C (325°F).

Flatten fish fillets by rolling with a milk bottle or glass rolling pin, and place in a buttered fireproof dish. Moisten with the wine or lemon juice, cover with a layer of greased paper and bake in a moderate oven for 10 minutes.

While fish is cooking, drain the spinach and chop it finely or rub it through a sieve. Mix with the cup of béchamel sauce and salt and pepper.

Cover fish with spinach and sauce mixture and top with breadcrumbs and grated cheese.

Place under moderate heat in griller until breadcrumbs brown and cheese melts.

Serve immediately with baked whole potatoes and sour cream.

Serves 4 to 5

Barbecued Fish

Kathryn Greiner was kind enough to give me this recipe.

catch of the day (jewfish cutlets are particularly good)

2 tablespoons butter

lemon juice

soy sauce

Place fish in centre of a greased sheet of foil with butter, lemon juice and soy sauce, to taste.

Wrap fish envelope-style before placing on the barbecue.

A crisp white wine is a good accompaniment.

Flo and Alice's Special Fish Dish

This is a delicious low-fat dish to salve your conscience when you feel guilty about all the wicked things you've eaten when you should have been worrying about your cholesterol level. I like to make double the quantity of sauce and put the extra in the refrigerator to eat later with plain grilled or fried fish which might be a little dry — it's just as nice cold as it is hot.

vegetable oil

1 large clove garlic, bruised

1 large brown onion, finely chopped

2 tablespoons tomato paste

500 g (1 lb) fresh tomatoes,
    peeled, seeded and chopped

400 g (14 oz) tin whole
    tomatoes, drained (reserve juice)

salt and freshly ground pepper

3 bay leaves, finely crushed or chopped if fresh

2-3 drops Tabasco sauce

1 teaspoon fresh basil, finely
    chopped (or 1/2 teaspoon dried basil)

1 capsicum, red or green, seeded and chopped

3 stalks celery, finely chopped

1 teaspoon sugar

2 pieces green or preserved ginger, chopped

1 cup fish stock or dry white wine

4 thick fillets fish (gemfish, snapper,
    jewfish or teraglin), skinned and boned

1 tablespoon dark malt vinegar

parsley

paprika

lemon slices

Into a large, heavy frying pan, pour just enough oil to cover surface. Rub bruised garlic clove well round the pan and discard (or retain and add to sauce later if you want more garlic flavour). Heat oil gently, add onion and sauté until lightly coloured.

Add tomato paste, fresh and tinned tomatoes, salt, pepper, bay leaves, Tabasco sauce and basil. Then add chopped capsicum, celery, sugar and ginger. Cook slowly, stirring, for about 15 minutes. Add juice from tinned tomatoes and fish stock or wine. Cook, stirring, for another 2 to 3 minutes. Add a little more wine at this point if sauce seems too thick.

Place fish fillets carefully in sauce mixture, sprinkle with vinegar, and poach very gently, uncovered, for about 12 minutes (depending on thickness of fish).

Serve immediately on hot plates, pouring cooking sauce over fish and sprinkling with chopped parsley and a little paprika. Garnish with slices of lemon and serve with creamy mashed potatoes. The success of this dish depends on it being served immediately – it's not nearly as nice if left in the oven to keep warm.

Serves 4

Gefillte Fish

This recipe was given to me by Vivienne Gershwin, a superb cook of Jewish food. For this recipe I think it is important to mince the fish by hand with a knife rather than use a food processor or blender, as the faster methods seem to destroy some of the flavour of the fish.

Sauce

3 large onions, sliced

2 large carrots, thinly sliced

1 teaspoon salt

½ teaspoon freshly ground white pepper

3 tablespoons sugar or to taste

water (about 4 cups)

Fish Balls

2 kg (4 lb) fish fillets, minced
    (bream, flathead or jewfish are all suitable)

3 raw eggs

3 hard-boiled eggs, roughly chopped

3 large white onions, roughly chopped

1 teaspoon salt

½ cup sugar

½ teaspoon freshly ground pepper

½ cup breadcrumbs

In a large saucepan or broad-based pan, combine sauce ingredients and bring to the boil. Reduce heat, cover and simmer gently while you prepare the fish balls.

Combine minced fish with raw eggs. Mince together hard-boiled eggs, and onions, salt, sugar and pepper. Mix together with fish and bind with breadcrumbs – you may need a little more or less than ½ cup. Taste to check that mixture is moderately sweet.

Moisten hands and shape mixture into 'balls' about 10 cm long, 5 cm wide and 2 cm thick (4 in x 2 in x ¾ in). Lower balls gently into simmering sauce, which should almost cover them. (You may need to add, very gently, a little boiling water to bring liquid to required level.)

Try to use a pan large enough to fit all the balls in one layer, and don't make more than two layers. Cover and simmer for 1½ to 2 hours.

Allow fish balls to cool in sauce before removing to serving plate and decorating with carrot slices from the sauce. Serve sauce separately – it will become jelly-like when refrigerated.

Serve cold as an entrée or luncheon dish.

Makes 16-20 fish balls

Fish Kebabs

An irresistible dish that is suitable either for a barbecue or a formal dinner party.

4 large thick fillets of fish, boned,
    skinned and cut into finger-length pieces

12 scallops

500 g (1 lb) prawns (preferably green), shelled

1 large green or red capsicum,
    seeded and cut into long thick strips

2 large firm tomatoes, chopped into wedges

melted butter, margarine or oil

Marinade

1 clove garlic, crushed

1 cup red wine

rind and juice of 2 lemons

salt

freshly ground pepper

Mix all the ingredients for the marinade. Marinate fish pieces, scallops and prawns for 1½ to 2 hours.

Thread fish, scallops, prawns, capsicum and tomato onto long skewers and brush with melted butter, margarine or oil.

Barbecue over hot coals or grill under medium heat till tender (about 15 minutes), turning frequently and brushing once with more butter.

Serve with savoury rice, and use the marinade as a dipping sauce, or use sweet and sour sauce (recipe page 150).

Serves 8

Blackfish in Mustard Sauce

When I was young, my parents had the lease of the Watsons Bay Baths, and at closing time in the evening when the blackfish season was on, the end of the baths would be packed with keen rod fishermen with their little baskets of green weed and wet sugar bags all ready for an evening's relaxing entertainment.

A fresh blackfish, cleaned, gutted and scaled, put on the grill or wrapped in foil over the barbecue is hard to beat. Most people who are used to cooking blackfish grill it or fry it. We sell a lot in our restaurant grilled, served with plenty of lemon and chips. Here is a new way of cooking blackfish that is very tasty.

Fresh blackfish has a rare and beautiful flavour — unique. Once you are accustomed to it, you will want to eat a lot more of this clean, attractive fish.

2 large blackfish, filleted, scaled, skinned,
    with the black that adheres to the wing rubbed off

2 cups white sauce (recipe page 149)

2 teaspoons mushroom stir-fry
    sauce (available at Asian grocery stores)

½ teaspoon anchovy essence

1 teaspoon mixed grain mustard

salt and freshly ground pepper

1 cup breadcrumbs

butter

grated cheese

Preheat oven to 220°C (425°F).

Separate the flesh of the fish from the bones and flake it. To the white sauce add mushroom sauce, anchovy essence, mustard, salt and pepper, and mix. Combine with flaked fish and turn mixture into a well-buttered casserole dish.

Cover with the breadcrumbs, dot with butter and grated cheese, and place dish in the oven. Turn heat down to 180°C (350°F) at the same time and bake for 15 to 20 minutes until browned.

Good with potato chips, potato cakes or corn fritters.

Serves 4

Stuffed Fish à la Remoise

My thanks for this French recipe to Mrs Monique Dircks-Dilly, wife of the former Consul General of France here in Sydney. Jewfish is excellent cooked this way, or 3 or 4 trout may be substituted.

5 tablespoons butter

1 onion, chopped

3 tablespoons chopped celery

375 g (12 oz) crabmeat, flaked

salt and pepper

1 cup fine breadcrumbs

¼ cup chopped parsley

1 cup cream

1½ kg (3 lb) whole fish, cleaned and scaled

½ cup champagne

1 tablespoon flour

lemon slices

Preheat oven to 200°C (400°F).

Melt 4 tablespoons butter; sauté onion and celery until transparent. Add crabmeat, salt, pepper, breadcrumbs, parsley and ¼ cup cream; mix well. Stuff fish with this mixture and close with toothpicks. Place fish in buttered baking dish and pour champagne over. Bake for 25 minutes, basting several times during baking.

Place fish on heated serving dish; reduce liquid in baking dish, add remaining ¾ cup cream and a roux paste (see page 152) made of flour and remaining tablespoon of butter. Cook, stirring, for 2 minutes, adjust seasoning if necessary and strain over fish. Garnish with lemon.

Serves 3 to 4

Baked Barramundi Fillets in Creamy Sauce

6 slices barramundi (or cod)

3 eggs, hard-boiled, then whites and yolks separated

2 cups béchamel sauce (recipe page 150)

60 g (2 oz) grated cheese

juice and grated rind of 2 lemons

1 teaspoon anchovy sauce

nutmeg

freshly ground pepper

dry mustard

paprika

Preheat oven to 180°C (350°F).

Poach the fish gently in water for 10 to 15 minutes, depending on the thickness of the fish. When cool, remove the skin, and place fish in a baking dish. Put aside.

Sieve the yolks of the hard-boiled eggs and add to the béchamel sauce with the cheese, lemon juice and rind, anchovy sauce, nutmeg and pepper. Put mixture in saucepan and cook gently, stirring thoroughly until it begins to thicken. Spread it over the fish in the baking dish.

Chop up the whites of the hard-boiled eggs, sprinkle with mustard and a small amount of paprika and spread over fish fillets. Place in oven, decrease temperature to 120°C (250°F) and warm through.

Mashed creamy potatoes mixed with finely cut cooked celery, onions and parsley make a particularly effective accompaniment to this dish.

Serves 6

Murray Cod

My thanks again to George Heydon. He says that Mr Wynberg, his old tutor chef, always maintained that Murray River cod was the third best fish in the world and that this simple recipe was the best way to serve it.

1 large onion, sliced

1 large carrot, sliced

1 lemon, sliced

1 bay leaf

1 blade mace or ½ teaspoon
    powdered mace or nutmeg

water

1 kg (2 lb) Murray cod, filleted and trimmed of fat

fried parsley (see page 84)

butter sauce (recipe page 149)

Into a large saucepan place vegetables, lemon, bay leaf and mace and just cover with water. Bring to the boil and simmer for 10 minutes. Place fish fillets on top and poach gently for 10 minutes.

Drain and serve with fried parsley and a little butter sauce poured over.

Serves 4

Baked Whole Cod

This is baked cod with a difference — you can cook it in the microwave.

1 kg (2 lb) fresh cod or haddock

juice of 2 lemons

2 oranges, sliced

2 tomatoes, sliced

2 onions, sliced

250 g (8 oz) mushrooms

½ teaspoon paprika

½ teaspoon dried thyme

¼ teaspoon freshly ground black pepper

3 tablespoons dry white wine

lemon wedges

No salt to be used when cooking in a microwave.

Into a glass baking dish, place the fish, which has been freshly washed and patted dry with paper towels. Squeeze lemon juice over fish.

Arrange alternate slices of orange and tomato over top of fish, then spread onion rings on top again. Arrange some of the onions and the mushrooms around the sides of the fish.

Sprinkle seasonings over fish and surroundings. Pour over the wine. Cook 5 to 7 minutes on high setting of microwave, remove from oven and let stand, covered, for 3 minutes.

Alternatively, cook in a conventional oven at 180°C (350°F) for about 30 minutes.

Serve with fluffy rice and lemon wedges.

Serves 4

Salt Codfish with Garlic Sauce

A delicious Greek recipe, given to me by Marika Harris. Try it for dinner, using Marika's recipe for taramasalata (recipe page 57) as a first course.

1 whole dried salted cod (or any salted fish)

1 cup plain flour, sifted

pinch pepper

1 teaspoon baking powder

1 egg, well beaten

1 teaspoon olive oil

½ cup water

extra plain flour

olive oil for frying

Garlic Sauce

6 cloves garlic

½ teaspoon salt

1 cup mashed potato

2 slices stale white bread

½ cup olive oil

1 tablespoon lemon juice

1 tablespoon vinegar

freshly ground pepper

salt

Soak the codfish in cold water overnight, changing water a few times. Prepare a batter by blending the flour with pepper, baking powder and egg, then olive oil and water. Cut codfish in 10 cm (4 in) square pieces, dry them, roll them in the extra flour, dip them in batter, fry until brown in olive oil. They should be cooked in about 10 minutes.

Remove from pan onto a hot plate or deep dish; keep hot in oven.

To make garlic sauce, pound garlic with salt in a mortar until smooth. Add mashed potato, continuing to pound and stir. This could also be made in a food processor.

Soak bread in cold water and squeeze dry. Add to potatoes and garlic, pounding and stirring again until smooth.

Gradually add olive oil, lemon juice and vinegar, stirring vigorously until smooth and light. Add pepper and salt to taste.

Spoon garlic sauce over hot fish and serve.

Serves 4 to 6

Fish with Vegetables à la Grecque

This recipe comes from my friend Mira Sawicki.

600 g (20 oz) fish fillets (perch or ling
    are good), cut into 4 cm (1½ in) pieces

salt and freshly ground pepper

plain flour

olive oil, for frying

300 g (10 oz) carrots, finely grated

100 g (3½ oz) parsnip, finely chopped

2 stalks celery, chopped

½ cup water

1 teaspoon sugar

250 g (8 oz) onions, finely sliced

150 g (5 oz) tomato paste

squeeze of lemon juice

½ cup boiling water

Season fish with salt and pepper and toss in flour, shaking off any excess.

Heat olive oil in a pan, add fish and fry until golden brown. When cooked, remove and arrange in a casserole dish with a lid and keep warm.

Preheat oven to 180°C (350°F).

Add some olive oil to a saucepan and put the carrot, parsnip and celery in with the water, salt and pepper, and sugar. Cook for 10 minutes or until soft. Add this mix to the fish in the casserole dish

In the meantime, pour 2 tablespoons of olive oil into a wide pan, add onion and tomato paste, a squeeze of lemon juice, salt to taste and ½ cup boiling water. Cook for another few minutes then pour the sauce over the mixture in the casserole dish. Cover and cook in the oven for another few minutes.

Serves 4

Baked Flathead with Ham

A delicious recipe from Dr Don Francois, former Director of Fisheries, New South Wales State Fisheries. He prefers to use dusky flathead for this dish, if obtainable. Choose a large flathead, remove the head and discard. Scale and clean but do not fillet. Cut in steaks; that is, leave the backbone in. This is also a good recipe for large jewfish and gemfish.

1 large flathead, cleaned, scaled and cut in thick steaks

melted butter

salt

freshly ground pepper

plain flour, to cover fish

4-6 ham steaks or 250 g (8 oz) bacon

Preheat oven to 180°C (350°F).

Carefully wipe the fish dry after you have washed it and cut it up. Place the steaks in a baking dish in which butter has been melted, and season with salt and freshly ground pepper. Sprinkle flour thickly over fish and bake in oven for 30 minutes basting frequently and occasionally sprinkling more flour over.

Cover the partly cooked fish entirely with thick slices of ham steak or bacon. Reduce heat to 120°C (250°F) and cook for a further 30 minutes or less, depending on the size of the fish steaks.

Serve fish on a hot dish with the strained cooking liquor poured over it and the ham or bacon arranged attractively around the dish.

Serves 4 to 8

This is a tasty dish which goes beautifully with hot, buttered garlic bread. To the garlic and butter add salad herbs, chopped green onions (scallions), a few caraway seeds and freshly ground pepper. Glaze bread with egg, milk or cream before popping it in the oven to heat.

Whole Fried Flounder or Sole

flounder or sole (1 per person)

plain flour

salt and freshly ground pepper

1 egg

cream or milk

oil for frying

fried parsley, to garnish (see note below)

lemon wedges, to garnish

melted butter (optional)

To see if fish is ready, test it with a fork. If fish flakes easily, it is cooked.

Scrape fish but do not skin. Wash and wipe dry. Leave in tea towel until ready to cook. Lightly dredge the fish with flour seasoned with salt and pepper. Beat egg with a little cream or milk and either dip fish in mixture or brush over with pastry brush.

Heat oil until hot. Fry fish until light brown (10 minutes should be enough), turning once. Remove carefully and drain on kitchen paper.

Serve on hot plates and garnish with fried parsley and lemon wedges. A small jug of hot melted butter is a nice accompaniment to the fish.

Mashed, creamy potatoes or French fries (chips) are generally served as a side dish.

Fried Parsley

To fry parsley, add a teaspoon of oil and parsley to a hot pan and fry quickly.

Whole Grilled Flounder or Sole

flounder or sole (1 per person)

butter

½ cup water

Select similar-sized fish if possible. If too large, cut through centre of fish. Do not fillet.

Prepare fish as for frying (see above). Score the fish (make two incisions across centre of fish) and rub some butter on top part, which has rougher skin than the underside.

Preheat griller until hot. Pour water into grilling pan – this will help to keep the fish moist during grilling.

Place fish in pan and put under griller on medium heat. Cook, basting a couple of times with butter.

A medium-sized fish should take 15 to 20 minutes to cook. Be careful not to overcook it, and do not have heat of grill too fierce.

Serve as with the fried version, but remember that extra hot butter makes it more enjoyable, as sometimes the flesh of grilled fish is inclined to be slightly firm.

Jim Doyle's Jewfish Deluxe with Spinach Cream

This dish is served on the Wharf at Watsons Bay — at the restaurant where you can actually drop a line and catch a fish or, who knows, a mermaid. (Are there any mermen?) The spinach cream can be made up to 2 days in advance.

1.5 kg (3 lb) jewfish fillets (bones removed)

water

dry white cooking wine

1 Spanish onion, or substitute, sliced

2 small carrots, finely sliced

2 sticks celery, strings removed

some herbs from the garden
    (e.g. a sprig of parsley, thyme, rosemary –
    if using dried herbs, use only a pinch of each)

1 bay leaf

freshly ground black pepper

salt

sprig of dill, fennel or parsley for garnish

Spinach Cream

½ bunch spinach, stems removed

2 onions or ½ bunch green onions (scallions), chopped

200 g (7 oz) butter, softened

2 hard-boiled eggs, chopped

I dessertspoon olive oil

1 clove garlic, mashed (optional)

½ teaspoon mustard (ready mixed, or mix with cream)

3 drops Tabasco sauce

juice of 1 large lemon or lime (and a little zest, if desired)

pepper and salt

To make the spinach cream, cook spinach leaves with onion in a small amount of water. Drain well, chop and allow to cool. (This could be done the day before.)

Make cream mixture by placing in a blender, food processor or mouli grinder the softened butter, hard-boiled eggs, olive oil, garlic (if used), mustard and Tabasco sauce. Add cooled spinach mixture and blend all together. Then add lemon or lime juice, and pepper and salt to taste. Chill until ready to use.

Cut fish into 4 pieces, place in a deep pan and cover with equal amounts of water and wine. Add sliced onion, finely sliced carrots and celery, herbs, and pepper and salt to taste. Poach fish gently for 20 to 30 minutes according to thickness of fish, basting with cooking fluid from time to time. Do not overcook. (Test with a fork – if fish flakes easily, it is cooked.)

An hour or so before fish is cooked, remove spinach cream from fridge and allow to soften a little.

Lift fish and vegetables out with an egg slice and allow to drain. Keep hot.

Arrange the 4 portions on warmed plates, surrounded with vegetables. Cover fish with spinach cream. Serve with small new potatoes, cooked in their skins, and a sprig of dill, fennel or parsley.

Serves 4

Spinach cream is also particularly good served with fillets of ocean trout, although it suits any fish.

Smoked Haddock with Poached Eggs

My thanks to Elsa Jacoby for this recipe.

750 g–1 kg (1½–2 lb) smoked haddock
enough milk to half-cover fish
4–8 eggs
1 tablespoon butter or margarine
parsley, to garnish

Allow a generous portion of haddock for each person. Place fish in a deep frying pan, cover with water and bring to the boil. Boil for 1 minute, then carefully strain off the water.

Return pan to slow heat with skin side of fish up and half-cover fish with milk. Allow to boil slowly for about 2 minutes, then carefully turn fish pieces over and continue to cook until fish is almost breaking up. (Cooking time depends on thickness of fish.) Lift carefully onto dinner plates and keep warm in oven.

Into the remaining milk in pan, break 1 or 2 eggs (according to taste) for each person and poach. When firm, remove and gently place eggs on fish.

Add butter to milk, melt quickly and pour a little over each serving.

Garnish with parsley and serve piping hot. A side salad goes well with this dish.

Serves 4

Smoked Haddock or Cod with a Rich Vegetable Sauce

I used smoked cod for this recipe, and although the fish was nice and fleshy, I thought it was much too bright a colour. So I washed it several times to lighten the colour and remove some of the salt.

750 g–l kg (1½–2 lb) smoked fish
2 tablespoons butter or margarine
½ cup plain flour
1 teaspoon mustard
pinch salt and freshly ground pepper
2¼ cups milk
2 bay leaves
½ teaspoon dried dill
½ teaspoon dried basil
4 drops Tabasco sauce
2 sticks celery, chopped very finely or blended
1 tablespoon finely chopped parsley
½ red capsicum, chopped very finely
2 hard-boiled eggs, chopped
paprika
sprigs of parsley, to garnish
lemon wedges, to garnish

Place fish in saucepan, cover with water, bring to boil and boil for a few seconds. Discard water, add fresh water and bring to boil again, this time boiling for 5 minutes. Remove from saucepan, drain and keep warm.

Melt butter over a low heat, taking care not to burn it. Add flour and mix until combined. Add mustard, salt and pepper then slowly add milk, stirring all the time. Add bay leaves and seasonings and keep stirring to prevent sticking.

Stir in celery, chopped parsley and capsicum. Add eggs to warm up. Have fish ready on hot serving plate and pour sauce over. Sprinkle with paprika. Decorate with parsley sprigs and lemon and serve with creamy mashed potatoes.

Serves 4 to 5

Indonesian Spiced Fish (*Ican Bumba Pedas*)

My thanks to Mr Rasjidin Rasjid, former Consul General of Indonesia, in Canberra, for sending me this recipe for one of his favourite fish dishes. The combination of these spices is hot and delicious.

Salam leaf is similar in flavour to a curry leaf, though it is a larger size. Salam leaves can be found dried in Asian grocery stores.

1 kg (2 lb) whole jewfish

salt

2 tablespoons vinegar

1 mandarin peeled, chopped and deseeded

1 cup oil

3 medium onions, finely chopped

10 cloves garlic, crushed

10 large red chillies, finely chopped

1 teaspoon shrimp paste (terasi/blachan)

2 large tomatoes, sliced, or 3 tablespoons tomato sauce

2 salam leaves (daun salam)

2 slices laos (fresh galangal)

small piece lemon grass (sereh)

Wash the fish thoroughly. Mix salt, vinegar and mandarin and rub fish with mixture.

Heat ¾ cup of the oil in a large, heavy frying pan and fry the fish on a medium heat until golden brown. Remove and drain.

Blend the onions, garlic, chillies and shrimp paste, or pound in a mortar. Heat remaining oil in pan and fry onion mixture until brown. Add tomatoes, salt to taste, salam leaves, laos and lemon grass.

Add fish to pan and simmer for a few minutes.

Serve on a platter.

Serves 4

Moroccan Fish

The nurse at our local dentist told me about a special fish dish that her mother makes twice a week. This is the recipe she gave me.

6 jewfish fillets

2 onions, sliced

5 tablespoons olive or polyunsaturated oil

1 small can tomato paste

36 olives

1 tablespoon chopped parsley

salt and pepper

Preheat oven to 180°C (350°F).

Place fish fillets in a heatproof dish on a bed of sliced onions. Add oil and tomato paste and pour water over until fish is covered.

Add olives, parsley, salt and pepper. Bake in oven for 45 minutes.

Delicious served with potatoes baked in their jackets, spread with sour cream and chives.

Serves 6

Mediterranean Stuffed Fish

3 cups fresh wholegrain breadcrumbs

3 tablespoons lemon juice

1 cup fresh orange juice

4 tablespoons pine nuts

6 tablespoons currants

½ teaspoon ground oregano

freshly ground black pepper

2 teaspoons butter or margarine

8 whole silver bream, scaled and gutted

juice of 2 lemons

Preheat oven to 180°C (350°F).

Combine breadcrumbs, lemon and orange juice and mix well. Add pine nuts, currants, oregano and pepper.

Melt butter or margarine in frypan and fry stuffing until lightly browned. Remove from heat. Fill each fish cavity with stuffing, packing in firmly, and secure with toothpicks.

Lightly grease 8 pieces of foil or baking paper with oil. Place fish on foil, sprinkle with black pepper and lemon juice. Cover and seal edges to form envelope. Place on baking slide and bake for 15 to 20 minutes. Serve with an assortment of vegetables.

Leatherjacket with Green Onion and Mustard Sauce

These beautiful, white-fleshed fish are really a delight to eat — that is, after the task of cleaning and skinning them is over. They are best cooked whole.

whole leatherjackets

salt

½ teaspoon dried basil or dill

2 bay leaves

green onions (scallions), chopped

celery, chopped

mustard to taste

butter

To make a fish stock, remove tails and heads from fish and place in pan with enough water to cover, with salt, basil and bay leaves. Cook slowly for 15 minutes. Strain, reserving liquid and put aside.

Place the leatherjackets in a well-greased baking dish and sprinkle with green onions and celery. Add mustard and pour the fish stock over.

Spread butter on each fish and cook in oven for 20 minutes, basting once or twice.

When cooked, remove fish and place on a hot dish. Strain liquid into saucepan and boil rapidly to reduce. Pour over fish and brown under a hot griller.

John Dory Fillets

1 whole John Dory or 4 fillets

salt, optional

1 bay leaf, optional

500 g (1 lb) school prawns (peeled)

2 whiting or red fish fillets

1 teaspoon anchovy essence

1 egg

salt and freshly ground pepper

1 tablespoon chablis or sauternes style wine

few drops lemon juice

30 g (1 oz) butter

1 tablespoon plain flour, seasoned with salt and pepper

parsley, to garnish

lemon wedges, to garnish

If you have whole fish, fillet and retain bones. Remove head. You can make a stock by boiling the bones and head slowly for an hour in enough water to cover, with ½ teaspoon salt and a bay leaf. Incorporate this stock in your sauce or refrigerate for use another day.

Preheat oven to 180°C (350°F).

Wash fish. John Dory fillets are sometimes large and should be cut down the centre. Remove any bones from smaller fish. Blend prawns and whiting in a blender with anchovy essence and egg or pound them in a basin. Spread the prawn and whiting mixture over the John Dory fillets which have been placed in a buttered baking dish. Season lightly with salt and pepper and moisten with the wine and lemon juice.

Cover fillets with buttered paper or foil, place in oven and bake for 15 to 20 minutes, according to thickness of fish.

Remove fish to a hot serving plate, taking care not to break fillets.

Melt butter in a small saucepan, stir in flour, salt and pepper to make a roux paste. Stir the roux into the baking dish being sure that the sauce is well combined and there are no lumps. Bring to boil on top of stove then pour over fillets. Garnish with parsley and lemon wedges.

Saratoga chips (very thinly sliced potato), fried very crisp in olive oil, are an excellent accompaniment.

Serves 4

Nanban Zuke

Another delicious Japanese fish recipe by courtesy of a former Information Officer for the Japanese Consul General, Mr H. Date.

mackerel fillets (or substitute gemfish or jewfish) cut into bite-sized pieces

cornflour

oil for frying

2 green onions (scallions), chopped

½ small capsicum, cut into thin strips

few slices fresh ginger, shredded

Marinade

2 tablespoons soy sauce

2 tablespoons sake (or substitute sherry)

Sauce

½ cup vinegar

½ cup sugar

⅓ cup water

1 teaspoon salt

1 tablespoon sake

1 tablespoon soy sauce

Combine soy sauce and sake and marinate fish for 20 minutes.

While fish is marinating, mix together sauce ingredients until sugar dissolves.

Remove fish from marinade and drain. Dust with cornflour, heat oil in pan and fry until golden brown.

When fish is cooked, place on a serving dish and pour sauce over fish.

Pour boiling water over green onions and capsicum. Leave for 30 seconds, drain. Combine with the fresh ginger and sprinkle over the fish.

Serves 4

David's Pickled Mullet

Thanks for this recipe to David Sinclair who, with his partner, John Morfesse, owns the Holiday Cottages at Goolwa in South Australia. David says that after a day's fishing the lowly mullet becomes a rare delight as the guests swap yarns about the one that got away. Never mind, he tells them. They'll come back next year and catch it — a kilo heavier!

1 kg (2 lb) mullet fillets, trimmed of little fins, etc

plenty of salted water

1 litre (2 pints) white vinegar

7 heaped tablespoons sugar (or to taste)

2 heaped tablespoons cooking salt (or to taste)

2 onions, sliced

3 cloves garlic, crushed

freshly ground pepper

handful chopped fresh dill

olive oil

Place mullet in salted water for about an hour.

Drain well, then place in a bowl and add vinegar in which sugar and salt have been dissolved.

Add onions, crushed garlic, lots of freshly ground pepper and dill. Mix well, then leave for a couple of days in the fridge.

Drain off liquid, pack into a jar with more sliced onion, and cover fish with olive oil. The fish are ready to eat after a few days.

Pickled Fish

*Lucila Maddox, a dietician, gave me this divine low-fat,
low-cholesterol dish.*

10 fillets fish (snapper, bream, jewfish), boned

3 cloves garlic, crushed

2½ tablespoons polyunsaturated oil

10 tablespoons fine carrot strips

5 tablespoons fine onion strips

2 tablespoons fine leek strips

1 tablespoon fine capsicum strips

2 tablespoons fine celery strips

1 bay leaf

2 or 3 cloves

1 teaspoon ground cumin

2 teaspoons ground coriander

½ teaspoon freshly ground black pepper

1 cup water

2 tablespoons lemon juice

1 tablespoon dry white wine

1 tablespoon white vinegar

orange slices and parsley, to garnish

2 tablespoons (50 g) gelatine dissolved
   in 250 ml (8 fl oz) water (for cold version only)

Preheat oven to 220°C (425°F).

Wash and dry fillets.

Brown garlic lightly in oil. Add vegetable strips, bay leaf, cloves, cumin, coriander, pepper and water, and cook for 10 to 15 minutes until tender.

Add lemon juice, wine and vinegar. Simmer for another 5 minutes.

Place fish fillets in a large baking dish and cover with the cooked vegetable pickle. Cook for 10 minutes in a hot oven, or cover and cook over a low heat on top of stove for 10 to 15 minutes.

Serve hot or cold (see below), garnished with orange slices and parsley. New potatoes and champignons are a good accompaniment.

If serving cold, add gelatine mixture at end of cooking time, allow to cool and refrigerate.

**Below: Running alongside two
golden labradors, Watsons Bay**

Mirror Dory in Celery Sauce

Mirror (or Silver) Dory has increased in popularity and, when in season, is an economical meal for all the family. Lots of cooks would probably fry them like any other fillets of fish but I think they need slower cooking with ingredients that bring out the flavour. The flesh and flavour is altogether different to John Dory, which is in a class all on its own — 'super' class — but I must admit we all enjoyed this dish.

4–5 medium Mirror Dory fillets (1 per person)

1 large can celery soup

milk

2 stalks celery

1 small onion, finely chopped

salt and freshly ground pepper

3 drops Tabasco sauce

½ teaspoon dry basil

1 tablespoon butter

1 tablespoon plain flour

1 cup milk, extra

1 tablespoon Worcestershire sauce

strong cheese, grated

paprika

parsley, chopped

lemon wedges

Wash and dry fish and remove as many bones as possible.

Pour contents of can of soup into a large wide pan, wide enough to poach fish, not forgetting to add the same quantity of milk, as per directions on can. Add celery, onion and seasonings. Cook slowly for 15 minutes, add fish and poach for 10 minutes, taking care not to break fillets.

Preheat oven to 220°C (425°F).

When cooked, remove fish from pan and place into flat baking dish. Leave celery sauce in pan ready to be thickened.

In saucepan, melt butter and add flour, stirring constantly. Add 1 cup milk and Worcestershire sauce. When cooked and thickened, slowly stir into the celery sauce in which fish was poached, stirring all the time. Cook for a few minutes. Pour over fish in baking dish, sprinkle with cheese and brown under a hot griller, or in a hot oven.

When ready to serve, sprinkle with paprika and parsley. Garnish with lemon wedges and serve with potatoes that have been parboiled, drained, cut along the top, brushed with butter and browned under the griller. Some fairy toast also makes a nice accompaniment.

Fairy toast? Most people know how to make that. I didn't once, so here is how, just in case. Bake some thin slices of bread in a hot oven until brown and crisp. You can store this toast for a while in an airtight container. Notice how every guest will keep nibbling at it and will finish up with more butter than toast.

Serves 4 to 5

Marinated Stuffed Mullet

Practically any vegetable can be served with this dish, because the sauce will go with asparagus, cauliflower and also mashed potato, if liked — especially delicious is cooked celery.

2 large, beautiful, fat mullet (see note)

I like to use canned, green French peppercorns in this dish. I use them a lot in fish dishes, and they also make a nice addition to meat dishes. Pound them in a mortar or flatten them on a chopping board.

Marinade

2 cups white wine

1 cup brown vinegar

2 teaspoons peppercorns, crushed

juice of 1 large lemon

1 teaspoon salt

1 large brown onion, sliced

2 bay leaves, crumbled

pinch dried basil

Stuffing

2 cups cooled, fluffy rice, seasoned
    with salt and freshly ground pepper

1 brown onion, chopped

pinch nutmeg

pinch cinnamon

½ green and ½ red capsicum, finely chopped

1 large stalk celery, finely chopped

1 teaspoon salt

1 large brown onion, sliced

2 bay leaves, crumbled

pinch dried basil

salt and freshly ground pepper

½ cup plain flour

1 egg

1 cup milk

dash Worcestershire sauce

dash Tabasco sauce

1 clove garlic, crushed or sliced (optional)

oil or butter

NOTE: Ask your fishmonger to fillet the mullet, or take the whole mullet, remove head, cut away from backbone and remove. This lets the fish open flat.

Sauce

2 tablespoons butter or margarine

3 tablespoons plain flour

pinch salt and pepper

dash Tabasco sauce

1 teaspoon mustard powder (optional)

2¼ cups milk or ½ milk, ½ fish stock (recipe page 41)

1 teaspoon anchovy paste or essence

paprika

parsley, chopped

lemon wedges

Mix all marinade ingredients together and pour into a flat baking dish. Place fish in dish and leave for 2 to 3 hours, turning fish as often as possible and spooning marinade over. When ready, drain off and discard marinade. Pat fish dry and remove black parts you may not have cleaned off. (Be careful with cooking after marinating, because the marinade partly 'cooks' the fish.)

Preheat oven to 220°C (425°F).

Mix together stuffing ingredients.

Grease a baking dish well with oil or butter. Flatten out mullet in dish and place some stuffing on each fish. Cover with well-greased foil and bake for 30 minutes in oven.

To make the sauce, melt butter in a saucepan over a low heat. Add flour and keep stirring until well combined. Add seasonings. (If you do not like sauce too hot, omit mustard.) Add milk slowly and keep stirring until you have a smooth, thick sauce (if too thick, add extra milk or cream). Add anchovy paste. This sauce can be used with any fish dish.

When fish is ready, remove foil and use egg slice to remove from baking dish and place on a serving plate. Pour over sauce, which must be very hot.

Sprinkle with paprika and parsley and decorate with plenty of lemon wedges.

Serves 6

Roly Pop Fillets

salt and pepper

2½ teaspoons sugar

garlic salt (optional)

1 brown onion, chopped

2 stalks celery, chopped

½ capsicum, chopped

Tabasco sauce

½ teaspoon basil

juice of 2 large lemons

1 medium can whole tomatoes
    or 500 g (1 lb) ripe tomatoes

plain flour

4 large, beautifully cleaned, fat-free mullet fillets

2 teaspoons arrowroot

1 tablespoon brown vinegar or lemon juice

2 bay leaves

1 tablespoon chopped parsley

Preheat oven to 180°C (350°F).

Sprinkle baking dish with salt, pepper, 1 teaspoon sugar, and garlic salt, if used.

Combine onion, celery, capsicum, dash Tabasco sauce and basil. Sprinkle over lemon juice, and add half the tinned tomatoes and juice. Add this mix to the baking dish.

Flour fillets and roll and secure with skewers or whatever you have that will keep them in place – even string. Add fillets to the baking dish as well. Cover with lid or foil and bake in oven for approximately 30 minutes.

Test fish to see if it is ready. If it flakes easily when tried with a fork, it is cooked.

Make a sauce of remaining tomatoes and juice, adding any extra juice from the fish. Put in a saucepan with arrowroot, remaining sugar, 2 drops Tabasco sauce, vinegar and bay leaves. Stir carefully and, when boiling, add parsley. Make sure arrowroot is cooked through.

Serve Roly Pop Fillets with sauce poured over and new potatoes garnished with parsley.

Serves 4

Pilchards Marina

In Theo Roughley's Fish and Fisheries of Australia (a most interesting book for any keen fisherman), he wrote: 'Much confusion exists in the public's mind concerning the relationship of the pilchard and sardine, and well it may, for the position is by no means clear. Originally the term "sardine" was applied only to young pilchards and a valuable trade developed in south-western Europe, particularly in France and Portugal, canning them in oil.'

Sardines or pilchards, they are delicious. This recipe was given to me by the secretary to Graham Jones, former manager of the then Sydney Fish Marketing Authority. He tells me that as well as being a great secretary, Marina is a great cook. After cooking her pilchards, I heartily agree.

1 kg (2 lb) pilchards, heads and backbones removed

salt and pepper

plain flour

1 cup oil

2 large onions, sliced finely

1 clove garlic, crushed

few pieces lemon peel

1 bay leaf

1 teaspoon rosemary or ½ teaspoon powdered rosemary

½ cup white vinegar

¼ cup water

Season fish with salt and pepper and toss in flour, shaking off any excess.

Heat oil in pan until hot, add fish and fry until golden brown. When cooked, remove and arrange in casserole with lid.

Add ½ teaspoon flour to oil remaining in pan (if too much oil, discard some) and stir. Add onions and fry gently. Just before onions begin to colour, add garlic, lemon peel, bay leaf and rosemary, and stir.

Mix vinegar and water, add to pan, bring to boil and boil for a few minutes. Pour this marinade over fish and, when cool, refrigerate for 24 hours, tossing occasionally.

Serves 4

I made this as an entrée for a small dinner party and served with it thin slices of bread baked in the oven until brown and crisp. It would be an ideal cold luncheon dish in summer with appropriate salads, especially lots of potato salad and hot garlic bread.

Alice's Sardines

You can either top the sardines with vinegar dressing (below) or use a simple dressing of pure olive oil, lemon juice, freshly ground pepper and salt and sprinkle over just a small amount of basil.

2 kg (4 lb) fresh sardines, cleaned, with heads and backbones removed (your fishmonger will do this for you)

salt

4 large bay leaves

4 sticks celery, finely chopped

12 black peppercorns, crushed

1 brown onion, chopped

½ lemon, chopped skin and all

On each side of backbone of sardine are fine, featherlike bones which should lift out with the backbone.

Put sardines carefully in a strainer and rinse under the tap, being careful not to break fillets. Place sardines in a large, heavy pan and cover with water. Add salt and remaining ingredients, slowly bring to boil, lower heat and simmer for 5 minutes. Cool in pan.

With a spatula or slotted spoon, gently remove sardines from pan and place in serving dish. (Be careful not to break the little fillets and leave the cooked bay leaves on them.) Strain stock and reserve for use in a fish or oyster soup.

Serve sardines with piles of hot finger toast, and garnish with parsley and lemon wedges.

Vinegar Dressing

1 clove garlic, crushed and chopped very finely

salt and freshly ground pepper

1 cup olive oil

½ teaspoon sugar

1 tablespoon chopped fresh herbs

2 tablespoons tarragon vinegar, or brown or white wine vinegar

Place garlic in bowl with pepper, salt and half the oil and mix gently. Add sugar and herbs, mix together again, add remaining oil and mix again. Finally add vinegar.

Place in a screwtop jar, shake a few times, and pour over the sardines.

Redfish Fillets

Redfish are commonly known here as 'Nannygai' (a lovely name — we all loved our Nannies). Select whole, fair-sized fish if possible, or if you like you can buy them already filleted direct from your friendly fishmonger — try to get them skinned, too. Remove bones if possible.

1 kg (2 lb) potatoes

1 onion, sliced

butter

milk

1 kg (2 lb) redfish fillets

butter

salt and freshly ground pepper

parsley, chopped

juice of 1 lemon

breadcrumbs

Boil potatoes with onion, and when cooked strain well, making sure they are very dry. Mash with a little butter and milk.

Cut fish fillets in two if large. Place in a buttered frying pan and season with salt and pepper. Sprinkle with parsley and cover with some melted butter or margarine. Squeeze lemon juice over. Cover with buttered paper and fry gently for 5 to 7 minutes – no longer, please.

Remove fillets and drain on a piece of kitchen paper. (Do not place one fillet on top of another.)

Place redfish fillets in a heatproof dish, top with potato mixture, dot with butter and sprinkle with breadcrumbs and freshly ground pepper. Place under a hot griller to brown.

This dish is good served with fresh green vegetables, such as zucchini, or fried red or green capsicum, chopped firm tomatoes and celery pieces fried together in butter for 15 minutes only.

Serves 4

Baked Snapper with Tomatoes

Thank you so much to George Andronicus (everybody knows Andronicus coffee) both for this wonderful recipe for snapper and for his help in putting this book together. (If snapper is unobtainable, substitute any whole fish up to 1.5 kg (3 lb) in weight.) George suggests his taramasalata (recipe page 57) as a good entrée to this main course dish.

1 kg (2 lb) snapper

2 cups chopped fresh tomatoes

1 cup water

4 stalks celery, chopped

2 teaspoons sugar

1 onion, sliced

3 tablespoons flour

¼ cup cold water

3 teaspoons butter

salt

paprika

parsley

Prepare fish for baking (see page 64) and place in a shallow baking dish. Put tomatoes, water, celery, sugar and onion in saucepan and cook for 15 minutes.

Mix flour to a smooth paste with cold water. Melt butter in saucepan and stir in paste. Add to the tomato mixture with salt and paprika.

Preheat oven to 170°C (325°F).

Cook for another 10 minutes, then strain and pour over fish. Bake slowly in oven for about 45 minutes.

Place on a hot platter garnished with parsley.

Serve with a green salad and grated zucchini.

Serves 4

Sole in Champagne Sauce

I am indebted to Mrs Monique Dircks–Dilly, wife of the former Consul General of France in Sydney, for this recipe, one of her favourites. Having made it, I can imagine if this dish is served, guests will be clamouring to be invited again. When fillets of sole are unobtainable, other fish, of course, can be substituted. Please be careful of bones — it is best to bone the fish before marinating.

If you have no champagne, use any sparkling cheaper wine or moselle.

6 fillets of sole or boned whiting

1 cup champagne

1 tablespoon lemon juice

salt and pepper

1 garlic clove, minced (optional)

300 ml (10 fl oz) pure cream

300 ml (10 fl oz) milk

Parmesan cheese, freshly grated

250 g (8 oz) white seedless grapes

1 tablespoon chopped parsley

lemon slices

Marinate fillets for 30 minutes in champagne, lemon juice and seasonings; add garlic if you wish.

Preheat oven to 180°C (350°F).

Remove fillets from marinade and wrap in foil or baking paper. Bake for 20 minutes in a moderate oven.

Make thin cream sauce by combining cream and milk and heating over low heat. Do not boil.

Unwrap fish and place on a heat-resistant platter. Pour cream sauce over, dust lightly with Parmesan cheese and place grapes around fish. Brown lightly to golden colour under preheated griller.

Garnish with parsley and lemon slices.

Serves 6

Susan Ranicar's Ocean Trout and Atlantic Salmon

At Long Bay, Port Arthur, we visited a fish farm operated by Piers and Susan Ranicar and their family, owners of Tasmanian Smokehouse Pty Ltd. They farm both Atlantic salmon and ocean trout, and we saw how the fish are grown in floating net pens. The nets float in 12 to 15 metres of water, each pen holding about 5 tonnes of fish when the fish are fully grown. The fish are acclimatised to salt water by being exposed to gradually increasing degrees of salinity until they are ready to be transferred to the pens.

Back at the Ranicars' lovely home at Deloraine, we had the most delicious lunch. I felt I simply must include details of it here — my thanks to our charming hostess for generously responding to my request.

The sight of beautiful deep pink salmon or trout lying on a big platter on a bed of fresh herbs, dill, parsley and coriander, garnished with slices of lemons or limes, is just superb. Here is Susan's recipe.

whole salmon or trout

sliced lemon or limes, for garnish

Stuffing

fresh dill, chopped

fresh parsley, chopped

juice of 1 lemon

glass of white wine

salt and pepper

half a clove of garlic, crushed

Preheat oven to 200°C (400°F).

Combine stuffing ingredients and stuff the salmon or trout. Wrap in foil and cook in the oven for about 30 minutes. Check during cooking, as it cooks very quickly.

When cool, peel away the skin, and it's ready to eat.

Garnish with slices of lemon or lime, and serve with homemade mayonnaise.

Serves 2 if a 1 kilo fish, or 3 if a 1.5 kilo fish (see page 31)

Susan's Mayonnaise

2 egg yolks

salt

1 tablespoon white wine vinegar

2 teaspoons French mustard

about ¾ cup olive oil

Place first four ingredients in a food processor and mix for a few seconds. Very slowly, drip, then pour, olive oil into it, mixing all the while, and adding a tablespoon of hot water if it gets too thick.

Tasmanian Salmon with Summer Salsa

4 portions Tasmanian Atlantic salmon

4 tablespoons very soft unsalted butter

Salsa

2 tablespoons unsalted butter

3 tablespoons peanut oil

2 small red onions, finely sliced

2 firm bananas, sliced

2 large mangoes, peeled and coarsely chopped

125 ml (4 fl oz) cup sweet chilli sauce

2 tablespoons caster (superfine) sugar

1 cup fresh coriander leaves, coarsely chopped

To make the salsa, heat the butter and oil in a large, heavy-based frying pan and add the red onions, bananas and mangoes. Sauté over a medium heat, stirring occasionally for 4–5 minutes, or until onion is soft. Remove from the heat and stir in chilli sauce, sugar and coriander leaves.

Brush the salmon portions with some of the butter and place under a medium to hot grill, skin side up. Grill for 5–6 minutes until the salmon is crusty on top, but slightly underdone in the centre. Brush with the remaining butter during cooking. Do not turn.

Serve the salmon accompanied by warm summer salsa.

Serves 4

Baked Ocean Trout

Lynne Allen-Brown, A.M., Director of Community and Hospital Relations, St Luke's Hospital, Sydney, gave me this lovely, delicate recipe.

1 large ocean trout (about 1.5 kg or 3 lb)

125 g (4 oz) butter, sliced, plus extra for oiling the foil

3 lemons

parsley

Preheat oven to 180°C (350°F).

Wash trout in cold water. Slice 2 of the lemons.

Grease a large sheet of foil or baking paper with some butter, place fish in centre of foil, and place sliced lemon around, over and in fish.

Place sliced butter over and in fish.

Wrap like a parcel, and place in another piece of foil. Bake in oven for 20 to 25 minutes, or until cooked. (Do not overcook.)

Serve on a large platter, decorated with parsley and lemon wedges.

If serving with hollandaise sauce (recipe page 152), be sparing so that the sauce does not overpower the delicacy of the fish.

Serves 3

Rainbow Trout

This recipe was given to me by George Heydon.

1 whole rainbow trout, cleaned

salt and pepper

lemon juice

butter

bacon lard or dripping

Rainbow trout are freshwater trout and, like most freshwater fish, are not as flavoursome as the saltwater variety. They make excellent eating nonetheless.

Season fish with salt, pepper and lemon juice. Butter inside of fish and smear outside with bacon lard or dripping.

Wrap tightly in buttered foil. Bake in a moderate oven or under griller until cooked (about 30 minutes, according to size).

When ready, unwrap at table to retain flavour and juices.

Serves 2

Trout Amandine

My thanks to Len Evans.

1 kg (2 lb) fillet of rainbow trout

salt and pepper

1 egg

1 cup milk

flour

½ cup butter

⅓ cup slivered almonds

juice of 2 lemons

2 tablespoons Worcestershire sauce

1 tablespoon chopped parsley

Season the trout with salt and pepper. Dip in batter of beaten egg and milk, then drain and dredge with flour.

In a heavy pan, melt butter and sauté trout for about 5 to 8 minutes, or until golden brown. Remove trout to a warm platter. Add almonds to pan and brown lightly. Add lemon juice, Worcestershire sauce and parsley. Heat through and pour over fish.

Serves 3 to 4

Peter Doyle Jnr's Trout Scallop with Ginger, Garlic and Tomatoes

This dish is served by my grandson Peter at Doyles on the Beach, Watsons Bay. It's a terrific recipe, as there is no need to cook the fish — the heat of the plate and the sauce cook it.

4 x 60 g (2 oz) slices ocean trout, skinned
    and boneless, not more than 5 mm (¼ in) thick

1 cup fish stock (recipe page 41)

60 g (2 oz) piece ginger, peeled and finely chopped

3 cloves garlic, finely chopped

⅔ cup tomato concasse (skinned, peeled tomatoes,
    cut and drained; canned tomatoes can be used)

6 teaspoons butter

salt and pepper

Preheat griller.

Pound trout slices until they are about 2 mm (⅛ in) thick. Pound from the centre outwards, taking care not to tear the flesh.

For the sauce, mix fish stock, ginger, garlic and tomato concasse in a pan. Bring to boil and cook for 2 minutes. Keep hot on a low flame.

Spread 4 heat-resistant plates with ½ teaspoon melted butter each. Place plates under griller until hot.

Season fish with salt and pepper and place a piece on each plate. Whisk remaining butter into sauce. Turn fish over on plates and pour sauce over. By the time you garnish the plates, the fish will be cooked.

Serves 4

Opposite: In the fish processing
rooms, Pyrmont Fish Market

Ocean Trout on Kumara with Couscous

Kumara is a variety of sweet potato and has orange flesh.

8 slices peeled kumara about ½ cm (¼ in) thick

4 portions ocean trout, skin intact

100 g (3⅓ oz) very soft unsalted butter

1 tablespoon lemon juice

cracked black pepper

250 g (8 oz) couscous

Boil the kumara in lightly salted water for 5–6 minutes until almost tender. Drain.

Arrange the kumara slices on a greased baking tray. Place the trout on the kumara, skin side up.

Combine the butter with the lemon juice and pepper in a small bowl and mix well. Brush the trout with the butter mixture and grill under medium heat, brushing frequently with the butter mixture until the fish is just cooked.

Meanwhile, prepare the couscous according to the directions on the packet.

Serve the trout and kumara with couscous.

Serves 4

Smoked Trout

1 whole rainbow trout

butter

pepper

lemon wedges

salt

Brine

1½ kg (3 lb) fine salt

500 g (1 lb) white sugar

1 teaspoon quick cure

30 g (1 oz) black pepper or crushed peppercorns

½ teaspoon ground allspice

½ teaspoon pimento

½ teaspoon cardamom seeds

1 bay leaf

11 litres (20 pints) water

Clean trout thoroughly, removing gills and point flaps. Combine brine ingredients and marinate trout for 48 hours. Hang overnight in smokebox (see page 64). Smoke for 8 hours.

To cook, poach in enough water to cover. When cooked, smother in butter and pepper and serve with lemon wedges. Taste before adding salt.

Fillet of Whiting Stuffed with a Mousse of Tasmanian Scallops & Served with a Light Lemon Sauce

This recipe comes from Gerard Catherin, head chef at Watsons Bay Hotel for 14 years. Gerard says this meal is 'inexpensive and delicious'.

4 nice, fresh whiting

300 g (10 oz) scallops with the coral (red part)

salt and pepper, to taste

4 whole eggs

250 ml (8 fl oz) full cream

lemon slices, to garnish

parsley, to garnish

Lemon Sauce

butter

half onion, finely chopped

¼ cup dry white wine

250 ml (8 fl oz) light or full cream

juice of 4 lemons

salt and pepper, to taste

Fillet each fish nicely to obtain 8 neat fillets.

To make the mousse, place well drained scallops into a blender with a blade attachment. Start the blender, add the salt and pepper, eggs and cream slowly. If you want a thicker mix, add a few little pieces of whiting. When mix has a nice consistency and is not too 'sloppy', it is ready. Leave it in the fridge for half an hour to firm.

Place the 8 fillets on a flat surface and pipe or spoon the mousse mixture on the widest part of the fillet. Then, roll the fillet up.

To make the sauce, in a frying pan, melt a tablespoon of butter, add onion, 2-3 spoons of wine and arrange the fillets in the pan. Put the lid on and cook for 3-4 minutes. Turn off the heat and let rest for 2-3 minutes.

Place the rolled fillets on warmed dinner plates. Place the pan back on the flame, and 2 nuts of tablespoons of butter and the cream. Stir with a fork and when sauce thickens add lemon juice, salt and pepper. Keep stirring with a fork for half a minute then pour sauce over the rolled fillets.

Garnish with lemon and fresh parsley and serve with boiled white rice.

Serves 4

Pan-fried Fresh Whiting

My thanks to Jill Wran, the wife of the former New South Wales Premier, and a charming hostess, for this recipe. With its delicate flesh, whiting is a great fish for pan-frying. The wholemeal flour gives it a nutty taste.

chillies, chopped

fresh herbs

olive oil

6 fresh medium-sized whole whiting

wholemeal flour

butter

lemon juice

parsley

Marinate chillies and herbs in olive oil for 24 hours to allow the flavours to infuse.

Wash and clean whiting thoroughly. Dust with flour. (Place flour and fish together in a plastic bag and shake.)

In pan, heat together butter and olive oil in which herbs and chillies have been marinating. Add whiting and fry, turning once and squeezing lemon juice on either side.

When golden brown and just cooked through (about 10 minutes), remove from pan and serve decorated with parsley.

Serves 6

Fish with Tomato and Dill

This is a quick and easy dish.

4 pieces thick fish fillet, about 180 g (6 oz) each

butter or margarine to grease baking dish

1 tablespoon lemon juice

1 cucumber

2 tomatoes, sliced

¼ cup fresh dill

½ teaspoon salt

black pepper

Preheat oven to 180°C (350°F).

Place fish in greased ovenproof dish. Sprinkle with lemon juice.

Peel cucumber, slice lengthwise, seed and dice. Blanch cucumber in boiling water for 2 minutes. Drain and place cucumber around fish. Top with sliced tomato and dill. Sprinkle with salt and a generous amount of black pepper.

Cover with foil and bake for 25 minutes.

Serve with mashed potato and vegetables.

Serves 4

Henry Newton's Baked Fish

The size of the fish you bake will depend on the number of people it is required to serve. The following recipe is for 4 or 5 people. Remember to leave the head on the fish.

2 onions, boiled and chopped

1 tablespoon dried mixed herbs

2 cups breadcrumbs, fresh

salt and freshly ground pepper

1 tablespoon chopped parsley

1 stalk celery, finely chopped

3 tablespoons soft butter

milk

2 kg (4 lb) whole fresh fish, cleaned and scaled

Preheat oven to 220°C (425°F).

Mix together onions, herbs, breadcrumbs, pepper and salt, parsley and celery. Rub in butter and moisten with milk till your mixture is firm and wet but not sloppy. Stuff the fish with this mixture and secure opening with coarse cotton or small skewers. In the opening behind the head, insert an empty tin or small heatproof basin to support the fish in an upright position in baking dish (as if it was swimming).

Carefully arrange fish in oiled baking dish and place in hot oven; decrease heat to 60°C (140°F) and cook slowly, basting now and then with a little milk. A 2 kg (4 lb) fish should be cooked in about 45 minutes. The fish is cooked when the flesh tends to come away from the bone.

When cooked, serve immediately. Gently place the whole intact fish on a large, hot oval plate, leaving enough room for you to pour over your favourite sauce. Potatoes baked in their jackets are a nice change, and they can be served in a separate dish with the baked fish as the centrepiece. It makes life easier if guests serve themselves, each one cutting a slice from the side of the fish.

This dish may also be served cold. Cook the fish earlier in the day and when it is cold glaze with a seafood glaze (recipe page 64) and decorate with lemon slices, fancy-cut carrots and olives, and so on. Accompany with potato salad and hot fresh bread rolls, either garlic or plain.

Serves 4 to 5

Fried Whitebait

Whitebait are tiny little fish — they say all good things come in small parcels. This recipe is for fresh whitebait. Let's wrap them up in an airy-fairy flour seasoned with pepper and salt. Pilchards could be used an alternative fish in this recipe.

fresh whitebait

plain flour

salt and freshly ground pepper

olive oil or other vegetable oil

lemon juice

freshly ground pepper

parsley

Make sure whitebait are free from sand and seaweed. Put into a wire mesh strainer and wash under a running tap.

Dry well on a special, clean fine cloth you keep for fish only.

Place whitebait on a sheet of white butcher's paper on your workbench, and sprinkle lightly with flour seasoned with salt and pepper.

Place whitebait in your wire chip-frying basket, place basket in deep, hot oil and fry for about 5 minutes. Drain.

Sprinkle whitebait with lemon juice and freshly ground pepper.

Serve with thin fingers of brown bread and butter.

Decorate with sprigs of parsley.

Char-grilled Tuna Steaks

4 tuna steaks

lemon wedges

Basting sauce

250 ml (8 fl oz) olive oil

1 tablespoon fresh ginger, finely chopped

2 small red chillies, finely chopped (or to taste)

1 clove garlic, finely chopped

3 green onions (scallions), finely chopped

3 tablespoons dry white wine

1 tablespoon sweet sherry

1 bay leaf

1 tablespoon caster (superfine) sugar

Combine all the basting sauce ingredients in a small saucepan and simmer over a low heat for 5 minutes. Discard the bay leaf.

Brush the tuna steaks generously with the sauce and place under a low to medium grill for about 5 minutes, basting often with the sauce. Do not turn. Steaks should be firm and pink inside.

Serve with mashed potato and steamed snow peas.

Garnish with lemon wedges.

Serves 4

Seafood

Seafood

Once upon a time 'seafood' just meant oysters, prawns, crabs and lobsters to most people. But these days, largely thanks to influences from Europe and Asia, a wide range of shellfish, crustaceans and other creatures is appearing in our fishmarkets: scallops, mussels, pippies, abalone, Balmain bugs, squid, octopus and cuttlefish (to name just some of these), are becoming more and more popular. In this section of the book you'll find good recipes for a wide range of seafood, and at the end there's a selection of recipes which are really 'seafood extravaganzas', using several different kinds of seafood — Doyles Paella, Seafood Omelette and Peking Firepot, for example.

The most important thing to remember when cooking seafood is not to overcook. The flesh is delicate and needs to be cooked quickly and removed from the heat straight away — not simmered until it is tough and stringy. And don't overpower the fresh, subtle flavour of shellfish and crustaceans by using strong sauces and seasonings — the natural taste of the fresh seafood will carry the dish, if you let it.

Prawns

As soon as prawns are mentioned, so is that old Australian saying 'Don't come the raw prawn'. So I certainly won't. These are all 'yummy' recipes and, if you are using cooked prawns, I think you had better have twice the quantity you need for your recipe unless you can find someone else to peel them for you. I'm a hopeless case myself – one for the pot and one for my mouth! When you do come the 'raw prawn', that's a different matter – I mean the 'green', uncooked prawn, with which so many dishes are made. They're harder to shell and devein, but they give delicious results.

How many of you have been prawning? Whenever it was or will be, it is one of the happiest times of your life. A great spot in New South Wales for prawning is Tuggerah Lakes, not so far from Sydney. I just love that place. To me it means Christmas-time and the school holidays, sharing houses, work done in a jiffy, Mums, Dads and the kids fishing, strolling, surfing, calm ankle-depth water for the littlies, and the smell of hot fish and chips everywhere. And prawns – no Lakes holiday is complete without that magic word. What's a mosquito or two on those hot, dark nights in the stillness of the lake when the prawns are running? And then home, all talking at once, with wet clothes, shivering too, happiness everywhere, big pots of boiling water ready for the night's catch, television forgotten, and the art of conversation returned for a little while.

Freshly caught prawns – a feast!

Cooking Green Prawns

Just say we have 1 kg (2 lb) of freshly caught prawns. (You may have lots more – I hope you do.) If the prawns are alive, put them into fresh water first and they will 'bring up' any sand, etc.

Have a big saucepan ready with about 2 ½ litres (5 pints) of water and bring to the boil; throw in a handful (about 2 tablespoons) of common cooking salt – the good old-fashioned salt. Please do not use table salt. The salt helps to preserve the prawns if they are not to be eaten straight away, and retains the heat of the boiling water. Small school prawns should be cooked in 3 minutes, the larger prawns in 4 minutes. To be sure, make a test: the prawns will come to the top of the water and float, which is a good indication that they are nearly done. Take out a prawn and hold it to the light. If it is cooked, you will see that the flesh has shrunk from the shell slightly, and the prawn looks opaque. Be careful not to undercook your prawns – you will know if you have because they will get a black look on part of the body when cold. As soon as you are sure the prawns are done, remove them from the boiling water and place in a big bowl of iced water to cool them.

Now they're ready to peel, devein and eat with vinegar or lemon and bread and butter, or in salads, fried rice, curry and all the other dishes that call for cooked prawns.

Skewered Prawns

500 g (1 lb) large green prawns, peeled and de-veined

2 large green capsicums

8 rashers bacon, cut into sixths

500 g (1 lb) mushrooms

1 cup vegetable oil

1 teaspoon salt

pepper

Cut prawns into quarters.

Wash capsicums and cut into 3 cm (1 in) squares. Alternate prawn, bacon, mushrooms and capsicum on 48 small skewers or round toothpicks about 8 cm (3¼ in) long.

Place kebabs on a well-greased griller. Combine oil, salt and pepper to taste and brush kebabs with seasoned oil.

Grill quickly, brushing with oil mixture and turning until cooked (10 to 15 minutes).

Makes about 48

Australian Avocado and Prawns

Here in Australia we have some of the best prawns in the world — many of them swimming in my beautiful Sydney Harbour. And in the Sunshine State, Queensland, they grow delectable avocados — soft, nutty and delicious. What a double.

16 large cooked prawns, peeled

4 small cupped lettuce leaves

2 ripe avocados

French dressing

salt and pepper

paprika

thin lemon wedges

thin tomato wedges

parsley sprigs

Put 4 prawns aside for garnish. Chop remaining prawns and put aside.

Take 4 individual serving dishes and put a lettuce leaf in each one.

Wash avocados and dry. Split in two lengthwise and remove the seeds. Put one avocado half into each lettuce cup. Pour dressing into the centre where the seed has been and grind over a little black pepper and salt.

Fill the avocado centres with prawns, pour over more French dressing then top each serving with one of the whole prawns kept aside.

Sprinkle with paprika, and decorate dishes with lemon and tomato wedges, and a parsley sprig or two.

Serves 4 as an entrée

Don't forget to keep the prawn heads and shells to make stock (see recipe for fish stock on page 41).

You can make these earlier on the day of a party, but please be careful when reheating them. Remember, preheat oven to very hot (250°C/475°F), then lower temperature to 120°C/250°F when you put the seafood in. Seafoods cook in a few minutes, and the prawns will be ruined if cooked too long.

Prawn Salad with Avocado Dressing

How we all love avocados, and how lavish we feel when we are able to serve them to our family or friends. A couple of avocados can go a long way when made into a purée to be used as a spread or dressing. My recipe for avocado purée follows, used here as a dressing for prawn salad. It would go just as well with a plain vegetable salad.

1 kg (2 lb) cooked prawns, peeled

lettuce cups

tomatoes

green onions (scallions)
    any other salad ingredients you care to add

Avocado Dressing

2 avocados

grated rind and juice of 1 lemon

freshly ground pepper and salt

1 onion, grated

¼ teaspoon paprika

½ teaspoon tarragon vinegar

1 tablespoon olive oil

Put lettuce cups on plates and fill with prawns. Arrange other salad ingredients attractively around prawns.

To make the dressing, wash the avocados and dry. Cut in half lengthwise, remove seed. Scoop flesh out into basin, mash a little with a silver fork or wooden spoon. Add grated rind and juice of lemon, pepper and salt, onion, paprika and vinegar. Mix.

Beat in olive oil with a wooden spoon, or purée mixture in a blender. Cover and refrigerate until needed. This makes 3 cups of purée.

Serve salads with dressing poured over or in a separate bowl so that guests can help themselves.

Serves 6

John Doyle's Stuffed King Prawns with a Rich Sauce

24 large green (raw) king prawns

beer batter (recipe page 62)

oil for frying

Filling

6 slices thick bacon

1 medium-sized tin spinach (the Hero brand from Germany is very good)

1 onion

butter

1 clove garlic, crushed

1 large egg, beaten

parsley

breadcrumbs

pinch salt

½ cup sultanas, soaked in wine and drained

Fruity Curry Sauce

1 small jar fruit chutney

1 tablespoon curry powder

6 fine green onions (scallions), chopped

1 small jar mayonnaise

1 egg white, beaten

Butterfly the prawns by cutting each one down to the start of the tail and gently flattening both sides. De-vein and remove the heads. Put aside while you prepare the filling.

Remove bacon rinds and chop bacon finely. Drain the spinach well. Chop the onion and fry lightly in butter with the garlic. Mix all the filling ingredients together, using enough breadcrumbs to bind. Fill the cut section of the butterfly prawns with the mixture, press the sides firmly together and put aside in the refrigerator for a while to firm.

Prepare the sauce by blending all ingredients together carefully, adding the egg white last. Serve in a large bowl or individual dishes.

When you are ready to cook, dip stuffed prawns carefully in the batter, and fry in your favourite cooking oil (mine is olive oil) for 5 minutes in a deep pan. Remember to have the oil hot, but not at boiling point or the prawns will cook outside first. Serve with fruity curry sauce.

Serves 6

These Stuffed Prawns are served with the most delicious 'dip' sauce. When the prawns are eaten, you can mop up the rest of the sauce with the remains of your bread roll. Filling, but oh-so-more-ish! Fattening, of course, but tomorrow you starve. So when king prawns are in season, treat yourself and the family. You all deserve it.

Pineapple Prawns

2 tablespoons vegetable oil

1 brown onion, finely chopped

1 teaspoon salt

freshly ground pepper

2 large stalks celery, strings removed, finely chopped

½ capsicum, finely chopped

1 cup tomato sauce

1 cup canned crushed pineapple

1–1. 5 kg (2–3 lb) cooked prawns, shelled

Heat oil in a large pan, add onion and cook until tender, being careful not to burn the oil. Add the salt and pepper, celery, capsicum, tomato sauce and pineapple and stir well. Bring to the boil, then reduce heat and simmer for about 5 minutes.

Add the prawns, mix well, and heat through, remembering that the prawns are already cooked so they won't need much time.

Serve over a bed of rice.

Serves 3–4

Sydney Harbour Prawns

1–1.5 kg (2–3 lb) cooked prawns, shelled

4 tomatoes, chopped

250 g (8 oz) button mushrooms

½ cup warm white sauce (recipe page 149)

25 g (¾ oz) butter

½ teaspoon cayenne pepper

1 teaspoon salt

1 teaspoon mustard

parsley

Put the prawns, tomatoes and mushrooms through a hand mincing machine or blender, or chop together very finely. If using a blender, be careful not to blend too long – just a few seconds will do.

Put mixture in saucepan with white sauce and other ingredients, except parsley. Allow to come to boil, then simmer for 5 minutes.

Serve over rice or noodles, and garnish with parsley.

Serves 4

Curried Prawns in the Old-fashioned Way

You will try to do an Oliver Twist act with this one, for sure.

1.5 kg (3 lb) cooked prawns,
    shelled (reserve shells and heads)

2 tablespoons butter or olive oil

3 large onions, chopped

4 small cloves garlic, chopped

1 tablespoon curry powder

freshly ground pepper and salt

4 large sticks celery, finely chopped

2 small capsicums, seeded and chopped

4 tomatoes, chopped, or 1 small can tomatoes, drained

2 teaspoons sugar

1 bay leaf, crushed

½ teaspoon dried basil

1 tablespoon tomato paste

2 cups stock made by cooking the prawn shells
    and heads in salted water or tomato juice or wine

grated rind and juice of 2 lemons

chopped parsley

Make stock with the prawn shells and heads (recipe page 41).

In a heavy pan melt butter or oil, add onions and garlic and fry until a pale golden colour.

Add curry powder, pepper and salt, celery, capsicums, tomatoes, sugar, bay leaf, basil and tomato paste. Cook slowly over a medium heat for 15 minutes.

Stir in stock, add peeled prawns and warm through. Do not cook the prawns or the dish will be spoilt. When dish is hot, stir through lemon rind and juice.

Serve the curried prawns on a bed of fluffy rice or with lots of fresh, crisply cooked vegetables, hot rolls or toast fingers. Garnish with parsley.

Serves 4–6

Fisherman's Wharf Garlic Prawns

Michael's special garlic prawn recipe — and a wizard at cooking it is his son Jim at our Fisherman's Wharf Restaurant, Watsons Bay. You can use this recipe as an entrée or as a main dish. It may sound like too much garlic and pepper but believe me it's not — the result will please you.

4 cloves garlic

½ teaspoon salt

2 teaspoons black peppercorns, crushed coarsely

2 teaspoons lemon juice

1 tablespoon brandy

500 g (1 lb) green (raw) prawns,
    shelled, cleaned and split lengthwise

olive oil

½ cup cream

chopped parsley

Crush garlic with salt, add crushed peppercorns, lemon juice and brandy. Mix well.

Place prawns in saucepan or in those heavy, individual iron dishes you can now buy to cook and serve garlic prawns in. Add garlic mixture and enough olive oil to cover and cook quickly until prawns just change colour. Stir in cream.

Serve hot and sizzling in small bowls garnished with chopped parsley.

Serves 4 as an entrée, 2 as a main course

Satay Prawns

750 g (1½ lb) green (raw) prawns, shelled and de-veined

2 tablespoons oil

3 small onions, cut into wedges

roughly chopped lettuce

Marinade

2 tablespoons satay sauce

½ teaspoon Chinese five spice powder

pinch sugar

pinch salt

chilli sauce to liking

1 teaspoon cornflour

1 teaspoon soy sauce

1 nip dry sherry

Blend marinade ingredients in a bowl. Add de-veined prawns, mix well and allow to stand for 2 hours.

Heat oil in pan, add onion wedges and sauté for 2 minutes. Add prawns and marinade and cook for a further 4 to 5 minutes. Place a tablespoon or two of water in the empty marinade bowl, swirl around and add to pan, if needed.

To serve, put a layer of crisp, roughly chopped lettuce (or rice or wild rice) on plate and spoon prawns over. Serve immediately.

Serves 2

Prawns à la Evans Head

My friend Nell from Evans Head sent me this recipe.

125 g (4 oz) butter

juice of 2 lemons

500 g (1 lb) cooked prawns

1 teaspoon anchovy sauce

2½ cups white sauce (recipe page 149)

cayenne pepper

lemon slices

Melt the butter in a pan with the lemon juice and then add the prawns and anchovy sauce. Allow to stand in a warm place for 30 minutes until a nice pink colour. (The lemon draws the colour from the prawns.)

Stir in the warm white sauce and add cayenne pepper to taste. Bring to boil, stirring, simmer for 2 minutes and serve very hot on toast with slices of lemon.

Serves 2

John Doyle's Mild Mustard Prawns

1 kg (2 lb) large green (raw) prawns, peeled and de-veined

150 g (5 oz) butter

1 tablespoon pure olive oil

1 tablespoon finely chopped white onion

½ teaspoon chopped garlic

1 teaspoon Dijon mustard

1 teaspoon chopped fresh herbs (basil, dill, oregano, or your own choice)

freshly ground black pepper

salt (optional)

½ cup brandy

½ cup cream

parsley or fennel, to garnish

If using dried herbs in this recipe, use only a pinch of each.

Cut cleaned prawns down the centre and open out butterfly-style, leaving the tail intact.

Melt half of butter and oil in a deep pan; add prawns, onion, garlic, mustard, herbs, pepper and salt (if used). Cook over medium heat for 8 to 10 minutes, according to size and thickness of prawns. Add brandy to pan; flame. Add cream, then thicken with remaining butter.

Serve immediately on very hot plates, garnished with sprigs of parsley or fennel. Serve with a crisp salad or wild rice.

Peter Doyle's Prawn Cutlets

Delicious prawn cutlets as served at Doyles on the Beach Restaurant, Watsons Bay. Customers keep coming back for more. This is Peter's own recipe, which he often uses at home as well as at work.

1 kg (2 lb) green (raw) prawns

pepper and salt

flour

water

oil for deep-frying

lemon wedges or cocktail sauce (recipe page 147)

The time-consuming part of making prawn cutlets is the preparation beforehand. Cut or pull off heads. Shell, being careful not to remove tail. Split prawns down back and de-vein. Wash and pat dry.

Open prawns out and flatten, using the flat side of a cleaver, a rolling pin or a broad-bladed knife. Season the prawns with pepper and salt and refrigerate, covered, until ready to cook.

Make a very fresh batter of just plain flour, adding cold water slowly and beating until you have a thin, runny batter, just like pancake batter.

Heat oil in a deep saucepan or fryer, which should be at least half full. Dip the prawns in the batter and add to oil, a few at a time. The prawns come straight up to the surface, and in a couple of minutes they are cooked. Drain well.

Serve straight away with lemon wedges or, as we do, with creamy, freshly made cocktail sauce.

Nothing to it – no secret batters, just the freshest possible batter, good prawns, the best of cooking oil and cooked to order, not reheated.

Serves 4 as an entrée, 2 as a main course

Caesar Salad with Prawns

2 heads baby cos lettuce

16 cooked king prawns, shelled, de-veined, tails intact

1½ cups croutons

3 rashers bacon, cut into strips and fried until crisp

shaved Parmesan, to garnish

Dressing

4 egg yolks

1 teaspoon Dijon mustard

1 tablespoon lemon juice

6 anchovies

3 cloves garlic

250 ml (8 fl oz) extra-virgin olive oil

250 ml (8 fl oz) vegetable oil

½ cup grated Parmesan

salt and cracked black pepper to taste

To make the dressing, combine the egg yolks, mustard, lemon juice, anchovies and garlic in a food processor and process until smooth. Drizzle the olive oil and vegetable oil into the mixture with the motor running. Remove and stir in the Parmesan. Season to taste with salt and pepper.

To prepare the salad, tear the lettuce leaves and combine with the prawns, croutons and bacon in a large bowl. Toss gently to combine. Add the dressing and toss it through to coat the salad.

Serve the salad in 4 large bowls. Garnish with extra shaved Parmesan cheese.

Serves 4

Honey Prawns

16 large green (raw) prawns, shelled and de-veined with tails intact

1 cup plain flour

vegetable oil for deep-frying

Honey Sauce

200 g (7 oz) unsalted butter

1 small onion, finely chopped

1 tablespoon fresh ginger, finely chopped

2 cloves garlic, finely chopped

1 cup honey

1 tablespoon soy sauce

2 small red chillies (or to taste), chopped

To make the honey sauce, melt the butter in a saucepan over low heat, add chopped onion and stir for 2–3 minutes until soft, but not brown. Add the ginger and garlic and stir until aromatic. Add the honey, soy sauce and chillies and simmer for about 5 minutes until the onion is cooked.

Dust the prawns with flour, shaking to remove any excess flour. Heat the vegetable oil and deep-fry the prawns until they just change colour. Remove and drain.

Pour the honey sauce over the prawns and toss gently to coat.

Serve hot.

Serves 4

This unusual way of preparing prawns has two advantages. Roasting cooks them with the shell intact and adds flavour, and it also prevents the delicate flesh from drying out during cooking.

Roasted Prawns

To prepare the prawns, use kitchen scissors to cut the legs off and then cut a slit in the back of the shell. Devein the prawn, leaving the shell intact. Prawns cooked on the barbecue are also delicious prepared this way.

12 large green (raw) king prawns, de-veined
    and legs removed, body and shell intact

1 cup cornflour (cornstarch)

6 green onions (scallions), finely sliced

Sauce

1 cup dry sherry

½ cup peanut oil

3 tablespoons soy sauce

100 g (3½ oz) unsalted butter

2 cloves garlic, finely chopped

3 tablespoons honey

Preheat the oven to 250°C (475°F).

Combine all the sauce ingredients in a medium-sized saucepan. Stir over a low heat until the butter melts and mixture is well combined. Do not boil.

Dust the heads of the prawns with cornflour and place them on a shallow baking tray. Spoon the sauce over the prawns. Bake for 10–15 minutes (depending on the size of the prawns), turning occasionally until just cooked.

Serve with steamed rice and garnish with green onion. Drizzle over some of the remaining juice if desired.

Serves 4 as an entrée

Italian Prawns with Fettuccine

500 g (1 lb) green fettuccine

2 tablespoons extra-virgin olive oil

16 large green prawns, shelled
    and de-veined with tails intact

1 medium red (Spanish) onion, chopped

2 cloves garlic, finely chopped

2 teaspoons capers

¼ cup lemon juice

100 g (3½ oz) unsalted butter, cubed

cracked black pepper to taste

4 medium basil leaves

4 thin slices lemon

Cook the fettuccine in a large saucepan of lightly salted boiling water until al dente. Drain.

Heat the olive oil in a large heavy-based frying pan and add the prawns, onion and garlic. Stir over a medium to high heat until the prawns just change colour. This may need to be done in batches, depending on the size of the prawns. Add more oil if necessary.

Add the capers, lemon juice, butter and pepper and stir until the butter is melted and the mixture is well combined.

Serve the prawn mixture on top of the fettuccine and garnish with basil and lemon slices.

Serves 4

Scampi

Scampi and prawns (or shrimps) are two different crustaceans. True scampi are small members of the lobster family, with thin and meatless nippers. These large scampi are caught off the continental shelf of Australia in deep water. Care must be taken when cooking scampi as the meat will break down and become soft with overcooking. Although they provide a small quantity of meat, what is there is truly delicious.

Deep-fried Scampi Tails

scampi
oil for frying

Beer Batter
2 large cups plain flour
1 can beer
1 teaspoon salt
2 egg whites, lightly beaten

To prepare the batter, put flour in a deep basin and add the beer slowly. Add salt, mix to a smooth, thin batter, and then add the egg whites. You may have to add a little more flour at this stage – the batter has to be well mixed and kept thin, yet retain 'body'.

Split scampi tails, flatten lightly, and coat them in the beer batter. Heat fresh oil in a pan until hot and fry in fresh clean oil for 3 to 4 minutes.

Chilled Scampi

scampi
olive oil
1 large red chilli, chopped
cooking salt
chopped garlic
paprika

Preheat oven to 220°C (425°F).

Split the scampi by cutting carefully down the centre to the tail, leaving the head intact. Devein with a sharp knife and clean.

Lay the scampi in a baking dish and pour over enough olive oil to cover. Add the chopped red chilli and sprinkle with cooking salt, a liberal helping of chopped garlic and some fresh paprika.

Decrease a preheated oven to 150°C (300°F) and bake for 15 minutes. When cooked, leave scampi in the baking dish and serve chilled in the natural juice they were baked in.

Hot Baked Scampi

scampi
clarified butter (see page 149)
1 teaspoon mustard powder
2 tablespoons olive oil
chillies
chopped garlic, to taste
1 cup Chablis (or other white wine)

Preheat oven to 220°C (425°F).

Split the scampi by cutting carefully down the centre from head to tail, and clean.

Place all other ingredients in a saucepan and bring slowly to the boil. Remove from heat, pour liquid into a flat baking dish and carefully place scampi in the dish. (This may be done hours before you are ready to cook.) Decrease a preheated oven to 150°C (300°F) and bake for 15 minutes.

The 'eye appeal' improves if you bake a long red chilli with the scampi and serve it on the side of the dish.

Crab

At one time we had a huge tank of salt water in which we used to keep some large crabs alive in the dining room of our old hotel. It wasn't a selection tank — it was just for the customers to see, and the children were always amused by it. It was a lot of work keeping the water clear and bringing up salt water from the bay, so eventually we put the crabs in buckets and took them down to the water's edge under the wharf, where they remained for a few days, and then they probably went out to sea with the tides to regain their strength. They were like your old pet duck or 'chook' to us; we could never have eaten them or served them to anyone else. Later on we used the big tank at our Wharf Restaurant at Watsons Bay, where it held an assortment of local fish. The children who fished down the wharf, including all our children, would come and 'sell' the fiddlers to us for the tank . . . it was fun.

I've had lots of fun with live crabs in my time, although when we have the mud crabs brought down from Queensland they are transported and securely tied with rope. Some of them weigh up to 2.5 kg (5 lb) and, being very much alive, you can just imagine the 'nip' they can give you (I mean the full measure, not half a 'nip'). Once, years ago, I had some smaller ones in the restaurant, and my young son undid the string and, much to the amazement and surprise of the customers and my horror, he let them go, to roam around where they pleased. You can imagine the laughter — and the time I had catching them.

Cooking a Live Mangrove Crab

1 live mangrove crab, about 1 kg (2 lb)

salt

water

When you buy the crab, it will probably be tied up with string to keep those nippers from nipping you. Place the live crab in the coolest part of the refrigerator (not the freezer). Crabs come from warmer waters of Australia and the cold makes them fall into a deep, final sleep. This should take from 2 to 3 hours, and then the crab is ready to cook.

Fill a large boiler with enough water to cover the crab. Bring to the boil. Add a large handful of salt — butchers salt or your plain ordinary cooking salt, not table salt.

Place the crab in water, bring the water back to the boil, then turn down heat so crab simmers slowly for about 20 minutes. When cooked, cool crab in a tub of cold water, otherwise it will keep cooking in the heat retained inside the shell.

Larger crabs will, of course, take a little longer to cook — use your own judgment here.

One 1 kg (2 lb) crab will usually serve 2 people

Preparing Crab for Salad

Slip a knife under the shell at the back of the crab and lift shell from body. Clean out waste under a running tap. Careful, otherwise you will wash the flavour out of the crab. Some people I have seen eat the roe and fat part from the head, others discard these.

Crack claws with a wooden mallet or small hammer. With a sharp knife, cut crab in half or quarters, remembering to keep head shell for decoration. To serve, arrange crab in its original shape on a large plate lined with lettuce.

The crab can be served alone, with bread and butter, or with a side salad or well-minted hot potato salad. A pair of nutcrackers or crab crackers, and a couple of long steel skewers to draw the last piece of meat from the legs are helpful. So is a large bowl to collect the bits and pieces of shell as the meal progresses.

One large crab serves 2

Cooking Blue Swimmer Crabs

Blue swimmer crabs usually die quickly after being caught so you must, if possible, cook them immediately. Place the very fresh (dead or unconscious) crabs in boiling salted water and bring back to boil. Cook, simmering, for 10 minutes. Place in cold water to cool down. Serve with bread and butter and lemon, or your favourite sauce.

Another good way of cooking blue swimmers is to cut them in two, dip halves into batter and deep-fry. Drain well and serve with lemon or cocktail sauce (recipe page 147).

Blue Swimmer Crabs with Vodka and Chilli

6 dried chillies (or to taste)

100 ml (4 fl oz) vodka

80 g (2½ oz) unsalted butter

1 white onion, finely sliced

cracked black pepper

4 green (raw) blue swimmer
    crabs, cleaned and cut into portions

4 green onions (scallions), finely sliced

4 fresh red chillies

8 chives, chopped

Combine the dried chillies and vodka in a small bowl and stir to combine. Set aside for 2-3 hours for the flavours to infuse.

Melt 50 g (1½ oz) butter in a large, heavy-based frying pan and add the onion and pepper. Stir over a medium heat for about 30 seconds.

Add the crab pieces and cook over a high heat until the pieces just change colour. The crab pieces may need to be cooked in batches depending on size. Add the vodka and chilli mixture, green onions and the remaining 30 g (1 oz) butter and cook until the juices thicken and reduce slightly.

Serve the crab and sauce with steamed rice. Garnish with whole red chillies and chives.

Serves 4

Curried Crab

1 large cooked crab or frozen crab

2 tablespoons butter

1 small brown onion, finely chopped

2 teaspoons curry powder

pinch dried basil

about 1 cup white sauce (recipe page 149)
    or crab stock plus about 1 tablespoon
    cornflour mixed to a paste with cold milk

salt and pepper

lemon wedges

desiccated coconut

Crack crab and remove meat (see Preparing Crab for Salad, 116), or allow frozen crab to thaw naturally. If you like, boil the shells with water to make stock.

Melt butter in a pan, add onion and fry gently until tender. Add curry powder, basil and white sauce or well-strained stock. If using stock, thicken mixture with a little cornflour made into paste with cold milk. The amount of liquid you will need depends on the size of the crab, so use your own judgment. Add salt and pepper to taste.

Do not overcook, remembering that the crab has already been cooked. Just heat through. Serve on a bed of boiled rice, garnished with lemon wedges and desiccated coconut.

Serves 2

Stuffed Devilled Crabs

This recipe is courtesy of Mrs John R. Davis, wife of a former US Consul General here in Sydney. It really is a super-delicious American crab dish. Thank you, Mrs Davis.

500 g (1 lb) crabmeat, flaked

4 tablespoons lime juice

2 teaspoons onion pulp

1 teaspoon black pepper

2 dashes Tabasco sauce

salt

3 tablespoons butter

2 tablespoons chopped onion

2 tablespoons chopped capsicum

1 small tomato, chopped

½ clove garlic, crushed

1 teaspoon chopped parsley

½ teaspoon dry mustard

pinch dried basil

pinch ground mace or nutmeg

2 tablespoons light rum

2 tablespoons fine breadcrumbs

cracker crumbs

Parmesan cheese

Mix the crab, lime juice, onion pulp, pepper, Tabasco sauce and salt and let stand, covered, in the refrigerator for a couple of hours.

Preheat oven to 180°C (350°F).

Melt 2 tablespoons butter in a pan, add chopped onion, capsicum, tomato, garlic and parsley and fry gently until soft. Add mustard, basil, mace, rum and breadcrumbs and stir over a gentle heat for 2 minutes.

Add marinated crab to mixture in pan and heat through, stirring well, for about 5 minutes.

Place mixture in cleaned crab shells or ramekins, sprinkle with cracker crumbs mixed with an equal amount of Parmesan cheese, dot with remaining butter and bake in a medium oven for 5 minutes.

Serves 2 as a main course, 4 as an entrée

Wok-fried Mud Crab

Blue swimmer crabs and spanner crabs can be substituted for the mud crab in this recipe.

Fish sauce is also known as nam pla *(Thai) and* nuoc mam *(Vietnamese). This salty brown aromatic liquid is made from fermented shrimps and has an unpleasant pungency which disperses during cooking. Fish sauce is available at Asian food stores.*

¼ cup vegetable oil

1 red (Spanish) onion, sliced

4 cloves garlic, finely chopped

2 teaspoons finely chopped fresh ginger

1 red capsicum, seeds removed, finely sliced

2 large green (raw) mud crabs, cleaned and cut into portions

8 green onions (scallions), finely sliced

¼ cup fish sauce

½ cup coriander leaves (cilantro)

Heat the oil in a wok and add the onion. Stir until soft, but not coloured. Add the garlic and ginger and cook until aromatic. Then add the capsicum and crab pieces and cook, turning occasionally until the crab changes colour. Add the green onions and fish sauce and stir for 2-3 minutes until well mixed.

Garnish the crab with coriander leaves and serve with steamed jasmine rice if desired.

Serves 4

Crabmeat with Pasta

4 blue swimmer crabs, cooked

4 tablespoons olive oil

1 medium onion, chopped

1 clove garlic, minced

1 tablespoon chopped parsley

1 cup canned tomatoes, drained and chopped

1½ cups tomato sauce (any bottled pasta sauce)

½ cup dry white wine

½ cup water

salt and freshly ground pepper

1 tablespoon sugar

½ teaspoon tarragon

pinch cayenne

4 tablespoons dry sherry

700 g (23 oz) spaghetti (enough for 4)

Crack crabs, remove crabmeat and put aside. Alternatively, you can buy the equivalent amount of crabmeat.

Heat oil in a saucepan, sauté onion and garlic until soft. Add parsley, tomatoes, tomato sauce, wine and water. Season with salt, pepper, sugar, tarragon and cayenne.

Cover and simmer for 45 minutes. Uncover and continue cooking for 20 minutes to reduce sauce. Add crabmeat and sherry; mix and simmer for 5 minutes.

In the meantime, cook the spaghetti until al dente. Add to the sauce, toss and serve.

Serves 4

Crab Cakes with Lemon Mayonnaise

Blue swimmer crab or spanner crab may be used in this recipe. Frozen crabmeat is now available at most fish markets, which makes this recipe quick and easy to prepare.

400 g (14 oz) crabmeat

⅓ cup fresh dill, finely chopped

2 small zucchini, chopped

½ red (Spanish) onion, finely sliced

1 tablespoon capers, chopped

1 tablespoon chives, chopped

1 tablespoon flat-leaf (Italian) parsley, chopped

salt and cracked black pepper to taste

2 eggs, lightly beaten

2 cups fresh breadcrumbs

vegetable oil for shallow-frying

extra fresh dill

Lemon Mayonnaise

1½ cups mayonnaise

finely grated rind of 1 lemon

2 tablespoons lemon juice

cracked black pepper

Combine the crabmeat, dill, zucchini, onion, capers, chives and parsley in a large bowl and add salt and pepper to taste. Add the eggs and stir to combine. Add the breadcrumbs gradually, stirring until the mixture comes together.

Shape the crab mixture into six cakes about 3–4 cm (1½–2 in) thick.

Heat the oil in a heavy-based frying pan and shallow-fry the crab cakes on both sides until golden and cooked.

To prepare the lemon mayonnaise, combine the ingredients and mix well.

Serve the crab cakes with lemon mayonnaise and garnish with extra dill.

Serves 6

Lobster (Crayfish)

We in Australia are lucky to have an abundance of crayfish (usually called lobsters here) in the sea surrounding our continent. They are big dollar earners for our country and are exported overseas, mostly from Western Australia. Most States/Territories have their own local species, which can be identified by shell markings. Some have a rough, spiky outer shell and when cooked are a bright red. Others, like the ones that come from the areas around New South Wales, are smoother and paler when cooked.

When selecting your crayfish (or lobster, whichever you like), remember that size for size, the female of the species has much more meat than the male, so it is heavier and the flesh is sweeter, too (only natural, being a female – now, now boys!). To tell a female? Well, look on the underside of the tail; you will notice that the females' fins are longer than those of the males, and they touch each other. Also, the back legs have a little 'finger and thumb' with which the female places her eggs in crevices and under rocks and seaweed.

Have you ever heard that yarn about the kids buying chocolate boys and girls (in my time they were about a penny each) and little Eva saying: 'Mummy, I want a boy chocolate, because you get a bit extra.'

In the crayfish line, the female has it!

Cooking a Green Lobster

To kill the crayfish (I always hated to do it and used to say, 'Please, God, don't let it feel any pain'), place it in a tub or large basin of fresh cold water until drowned. If your green crayfish is already dead, please make sure it is very fresh.

Place a good handful of common cooking salt – not table salt – in a big pot of boiling water. Cut up and add lemon, a large onion, a stick of celery, carrot – then in goes the crayfish. This crayfish water makes good stock for all seafood dishes. If you only want the crayfish cooked and do not need stock, just add a handful of white sugar with the salt and forget about putting in the vegetables.

A 1 kg (2 lb) crayfish should take altogether about 15 to 20 minutes' gentle boiling. If you have only a small crayfish, 12 minutes will be enough. Remember that crayfish lose weight when boiled, and overcooking will toughen and cause greater weight loss.

Lift crayfish out with tongs and bend the tail backwards and forwards. It should be pliable and return to the curled position. Place crayfish in cool running water.

Well, that's how it's done, though I suppose you will probably mostly buy cooked crayfish (lobster) from your fishmonger. After all, look at all the time you will save and, if you feel like I do, you will hate to kill them.

Serves 1-2

Lobster Newburg

1 cooked crayfish (lobster), cut in half

¼ cup white wine

½ cup madeira

1¼ cups thick cream

½ cup mushrooms, chopped

salt

dash Tabasco sauce

yolks of 2 eggs

lemon slices

Remove flesh from crayfish; place shells in oven to heat.

Place wine and madeira in saucepan, heat and simmer for about 3 minutes. Add lobster meat, heat through.

Add cream, mushrooms, salt and Tabasco sauce, stirring. Cook for a few minutes until all is combined and hot. When ready to serve, stir through egg yolks. Heat – but careful, do not boil.

Fill hot crayfish or lobster shells and serve with boiled, seasoned fluffy rice, sprinkled over with paprika. Garnish with lemon slices and, of course, all fish dishes must be served on a very warm plate.

Serves 2

Hot, Mouth-watering, Buttered Lobster

So, you have your own lobster trap, or perhaps you are away on a seaside holiday and you are down the wharf when the crayfish fishermen come in, and you have a beautiful, freshly caught crayfish . . .

Refer to my instructions for cooking fresh lobster (see page 120); don't run cooked lobster under cold water. Remove from boiler and split down centre. Have hot clarified butter (see page 149) melted ready, plenty of it, and freshly ground pepper and salt.

Put on a large bib, start off with a knife and fork, finish with our natural tools – hands, fingers and thumbs – then your little hammer or nutcrackers and a steel skewer for the succulent parts of the claws.

If you wish, add plenty of lemon wedges. Personally, I just like the flavour of the crayfish, the hot butter, pepper and salt.

A great meal will be had by all!

Lobster Mornay

1 cooked crayfish (lobster)

butter

2 green onions (scallions), chopped

1 bay leaf, crushed

½ cup white wine (optional)

2 cups white sauce (recipe page 149)

tasty cheese, grated

breadcrumbs

If you are feeling rather 'lush' and extravagant, buy a 1 kg (2 lb) or slightly larger crayfish. Cut in half. Remove the flesh and slice in scallops. Pop the empty shells (the two halves) in a hot oven (220°C/425°F) to get really hot.

Sauté the crayfish meat in a little butter with chopped green onion and a crushed bay leaf, and then add a little white wine, if you wish. After the wine has evaporated, add your white sauce and reheat.

Have the griller nice and hot, bring out the crayfish shells from the oven, pop your crayfish mixture in, place some cheese and breadcrumbs on top, and slide under the griller. Brown all over but please be careful and do not burn. Haven't got a griller good enough? Well, try the hot oven, although it's too slow for my liking and doesn't brown well enough. This dish is 'a touch of class' and deserves to be the best. I hope you and the family, or your guests, thoroughly enjoy it.

Serves 2

Delicious Grilled Lobster

1 green (raw) crayfish (lobster) split in
    half or two frozen lobster tails

dash of Tabasco sauce

liberal amount of butter

sprinkle paprika

little salt (optional)

lemon juice

hot melted butter

freshly ground black pepper

Make sure your uncooked lobster is fresh and has been cleaned correctly after being cut in two. If using a frozen crayfish, be sure to defrost naturally.

Chop flesh of crayfish while still in shell. Sprinkle a dash of Tabasco sauce over each half. Add generous dabs of butter, both over and under flesh. Sprinkle over paprika, a little salt if liked (not really necessary) and a squeeze of lemon juice.

Thus prepared, place the two halves on a tin plate or grilling tray, and put under a medium griller, basting frequently and turning over the flesh. It should be cooked in 20 minutes.

Serve your Grilled Lobsters with a small container of hot, melted butter and make sure you have your pepper grinder for fresh pepper ready.

I find this dish goes particularly well served with whole potatoes that have been carefully boiled, then strained, split at the top as though making chips but not cut through, brushed over with melted butter and put under a hot griller to brown and dry out. In fact, this is a delicious way of doing potatoes with any dish, meat or fish.

Serves 2

Curried Lobster

1 cooked crayfish (lobster)

3 tablespoons butter

1 clove garlic, crushed

1 brown onion, finely chopped

1 stalk celery, strings removed, finely chopped

2 teaspoons curry powder

salt

2 teaspoons sugar

2½ cups milk mixed with 2½ cups fish stock (recipe
    page 41) or water

2 teaspoons cornflour mixed to a paste with a little water

breadcrumbs

Cut the crayfish in half, remove flesh and slice. Place shells in the oven to heat.

In a saucepan, mix 1 tablespoon butter, garlic, onion, celery, curry powder and salt to taste. Stir until onion is tender.

Add sugar, milk and stock, and cornflour paste; heat, stirring, until mixture boils and thickens slightly.

Add crayfish slices and heat through. Pile the mixture into heated shells, dot with remaining butter, sprinkle with breadcrumbs and brown under the griller.

What to serve with it? Naturally, fluffy rice, lemon slices and maybe a fruity chutney. You know by now that eye appeal always does the trick, and it's very handy to have a parsley garden. You can always use a substitute for parsley when it is hard to obtain – try chopped up celery tops.

Serves 2

Lobster and Avocado Sandwich

8 thick slices grained bread

½ cup mayonnaise

1 large cooked lobster tail, sliced

8 bacon rashers, grilled until crisp

2 ripe avocados, peeled and sliced

4 crisp lettuce leaves

Toast the bread and spread one side of each slice with mayonnaise. Layer lobster, bacon, avocado slices and lettuce on four slices of warm toast and top with remaining slices of toast.

Serves 4

Spring Lobster

This delicious, low–fat recipe for crayfish comes from Lucila Maddox, the former dietician at St Luke's Hospital. Lucila was born in Peru and did her training in Buenos Aires.

1 cooked crayfish (lobster), sliced

2 avocados, sliced

10 artichoke hearts

10 slices pineapple

1 lettuce, shredded

4 slices lemon

walnut halves to garnish (about 20)

Dressing

1 tablespoon sunflower oil

3-4 tablespoons plain non-fat yoghurt (or blend of 1 part skim milk to 2 parts low-fat ricotta cheese)

juice of 2 lemons

salt and freshly ground pepper to taste

On a large platter, arrange crayfish, avocado, artichoke hearts and pineapple slices.

Add a border of shredded lettuce and place lemon slices around the plate. Spread with walnut halves and pour over the dressing.

To make the dressing, whisk the oil, yoghurt and lemon juice together in a bowl. Add salt and pepper to taste and mix through.

Serves 10 as an entrée or buffet dish

Lobster in Aspic

2 ½ cups aspic jelly (see below)

flesh from 2 kg (4 lb) crayfish (lobster), cut into neat pieces

3 hard-boiled eggs, sliced

celery (kept from aspic stock, see below)

1 carrot, scraped and grated

freshly ground pepper and salt

a few tarragon leaves (easy to grow)

6 capers

1 large lettuce

stoned olives, black or stuffed

oil and vinegar

mayonnaise

For Aspic Jelly

shell from crayfish, and other fishbones

seasonings

onion

1 stalk celery

herbs

salt

water

1 tablespoon gelatine

Pour some aspic in a mould or dish to a depth of about 5 mm (¼ in) and, when it is beginning to set, arrange over it in a pattern the crayfish, hard-boiled egg slices, some of the celery that was cooked in the aspic stock (sliced) and grated carrot.

Add pepper and salt and rest of crayfish and aspic, also tarragon leaves and capers. Place mould in the refrigerator to set. When set, turn out of mould, arrange on a bed of lettuce leaves, garnish with olives.

Whisk olive oil and vinegar with pepper and salt to make a dressing. When ready to serve, pour dressing over the aspic or you may prefer to serve separately.

Mayonnaise also adds to this dish, served with extra lettuce and tomatoes.

To make the aspic jelly, I take the crayfish shell and any fish bones I have, put all in a saucepan with seasonings, onion, celery, herbs, salt and water to just cover, and cook for 15 minutes. I then strain it into a bowl and, depending on how much aspic I want to make, I add gelatine. For this recipe I dissolve 2 teaspoons in 2½ cups of stock.

Serves 4-5

Balmain Bugs

I think the flesh of these cute little Balmain bugs is really delectable. Though it is much more tender than lobster meat, the proportion of shell to flesh is much higher, and you may prefer to buy your bugs cooked, when they are in season, from your favourite fish shop, rather than spend a lot of time preparing them.

Balmain bugs are often called shovel-nosed lobsters because of the shape of their heads. They are very similar to Moreton Bay bugs, with white flesh and a good sea flavour. Smaller than lobsters, they are actually a species of sand lobster and have no claws.

You can pop them on the barbecue or under the griller. They can also be poached or pan-fried. And they're extra good in salads.

If you want to make an impression, try the recipe for Balmain Bugs and Seafood Supreme. It's a family favourite, and you can vary the amount of prawns and fish that you cook with it, or perhaps experiment with other types of seafood in season. Makes my mouth water just thinking about it.

Balmain bugs have a strong iodine taste at times. You can eliminate this by removing the heads before cooking, if you wish. I generally keep the water from the seafoods I cook for stock, but the water in which Balmain bugs have been cooked has a very strong flavour, so I discard it.

Balmain Bug Salad

1 small red onion, finely chopped
½ cup extra-virgin olive oil
1 tablespoon raspberry vinegar
1 tablespoon Dijon mustard
1 tablespoon caster (superfine) sugar
salt and pepper to taste
16 cooked Balmain bugs, halved and de-veined
160 g mixed green salad leaves

Combine the red onion, olive oil, vinegar, mustard and sugar in a small bowl. Add the salt and pepper and mix well. Drizzle the mixture over the bugs and toss gently to coat.
Arrange the salad leaves on serving plates and top with Balmain bugs.
Serves 4

Cooking Green Balmain Bugs

12 green Balmain bugs
water
½ cup sugar
½ teaspoon dried herbs

If the bugs are alive, prepare for cooking as for lobsters (see page 120). Put enough water in a saucepan to cover the bugs. Add sugar and herbs. Bring water to the boil, add the bugs and cook for 10 minutes.
Remove bugs from boiling water and plunge into cold water to stop the cooking process. They are delicious eaten freshly cooked with lemon, vinegar and your favourite sauce.
Serves 4

Balmain Bugs, Fish and Prawns in a Sauternes Sauce

This dish is a 'special' in our family whenever Balmain bugs are available.

8 green (raw) Balmain bugs

125 g (4 oz) butter

1 large brown onion, finely chopped

2 sticks celery, strings removed, finely chopped

freshly ground pepper

salt

2 drops Tabasco sauce

1 large clove garlic, crushed

1 green or red capsicum, finely chopped

500 g (1 lb) filleted skinned fish,
    boned and cut into small pieces

500 g (1 lb) green (raw)
    prawns, shelled and de-veined

½ bottle Sauternes style wine

1 teaspoon sugar

Prepare the uncooked bugs by splitting in two; clean out debris from the head.

In a large, heavy pan, melt butter, then add onion, celery, pepper and salt, basil, Tabasco sauce, garlic and capsicum; cook slowly for 15 minutes. Add bugs, fish and prawns and cook carefully for a further 10 minutes.

Add wine and sugar, stir and bring to boil again for 5 minutes.

Serve in bowls with hot garlic bread or toast topped with melted cheddar cheese and sprinkled with paprika.

Serves 4

Balmain Bugs and Snow Pea Salad

Compliments, Chef Ian Meredith.

8 medium green (raw) Balmain bugs

vegetable oil for shallow-frying

4 sprigs fresh dill, for garnish

Marinade

2 cloves garlic, finely chopped

1 teaspoon finely chopped fresh ginger

⅓ cup honey

⅓ cup finely chopped fresh dill

⅓ cup soy sauce

2 cups water

Dressing

1 cup mayonnaise

½ cup pouring cream

1 teaspoon ground cumin

finely grated rind from 1 orange

4 tablespoons fresh orange juice

salt and pepper to taste

Salad

200 g (7 oz) snow peas (mangetout), blanched

200 g (7 oz) green beans, blanched and cut
    in 6 cm (3 in) slices

1 large red capsicum, roasted, peeled and sliced

1 large eggplant, sliced into ½ cm (¼ in) thick pieces,
    brushed with olive oil and grilled

Combine all the marinade ingredients in a container large enough to hold the Balmain bugs. Stir well. Add the bugs. Rest, covered, in the refrigerator for 2–4 hours, turning occasionally. Remove and drain. Cut bugs in half lengthways.

Heat the vegetable oil in a large heavy-based pan and shallow-fry the bugs in batches until just cooked. Drain.

To prepare the dressing, combine all ingredients in a bowl and stir until smooth.

To prepare the salad, place the ingredients in a large bowl and toss gently to combine.

To serve, arrange the salad on 4 plates. Top with the Balmain bugs and drizzle with the mayonnaise dressing. Garnish with dill.

Serves 4

Once you've roasted the capsicum under a hot griller or in the oven until the skin is blackened, place the capsicum in a brown paper or plastic bag for a while to sweat. Then peel away the skin and rinse under water if necessary to remove all the black.

Oysters

Oysters the Natural Way

Our favourite way – and, as I write, I've just had some for lunch!

Allow from 6 to 12 oysters per person if you are using them for an entrée. If the oysters have not been opened, open them and see that the shells are cleaned and that no pieces of shell are penetrating the oysters.

Wash carefully, but please do not wash and wash the oysters under a running tap. Retain as much of the oyster's natural juice as you can. If you have bought the oysters already opened, they will probably be okay, and won't need washing. Do not leave open oysters uncovered in the refrigerator as this tends to dry them out and a film forms over the oyster flesh. Cover oysters with wet greaseproof paper if you are not intending to use them for a while. Be careful not to make the oysters too cold. The flavour is gone if you do.

Serve on special oyster plates (these have a recess or fixed cup in the centre for sauce) or on ordinary dinner plates with small containers to hold sauces in the centre. Vinegar, tartare sauce (recipe page 147) and cocktail sauce (recipe page 147) are just a few of the many sauces you can use.

Serve the oysters with lemon wedges, freshly ground pepper and salt, and thin brown bread and butter.

Oysters Kilpatrick

24 oysters on the shell

1 teaspoon Worcestershire sauce

1 cup cream

pepper and salt

250 g (½ lb) bacon rashers, finely chopped

fine breadcrumbs

Oysters Kilpatrick are tasty served with a bowl of hot puréed spinach and thin slices of buttered brown or rye bread.

Remove oysters from shells and put aside. Put shells on a baking sheet and heat in a moderate oven. Mix Worcestershire sauce and cream. When shells are hot, return oysters to shells. Use tongs to handle the shells, as they get very hot. Add a little of the cream mixture to each shell; sprinkle with pepper and salt.

Top each oyster with chopped bacon and fine breadcrumbs. Place baking sheet under a hot griller and grill until bacon is crisp but not burnt and oysters are warmed through.

Serves 2–4 as an entrée

Fried Oysters

24 oysters on the shell

1 egg

2 tablespoons cream

plain flour seasoned with pepper and salt

Sao biscuit crumbs, crushed finely

butter

lemon wedges

parsley

Remove oysters from shell. Place shells on a large baking dish in oven to heat. Beat egg and cream together in a bowl. Coat oysters with seasoned flour, then dip in egg mixture, and lastly coat all over with biscuit crumbs. If you wish, you can place these crumbed oysters in the coldest part of the fridge for half an hour to harden.

When ready to cook, melt butter; it burns easily, so use a low heat please. Place oysters in and cook slowly until the coating is crisp, about 7 minutes. Drain.

Remove shells from oven (careful of burnt fingers – use tongs). Place oysters in the shells and arrange on plates. Garnish plates with lemon wedges and parsley and serve.

I have warned you, they are very more-ish.

Serves 4 as an entrée, 2 as a main course

Oysters Rockefeller

24 oysters on the shell

2 tablespoons butter

1 large clove garlic, crushed

3 stalks crisp celery, strings removed, finely chopped

½ large red capsicum or 1 small one, finely chopped

freshly ground pepper and salt

250 g (8 oz) bacon, rind removed, chopped

pinch cayenne

1½ cups breadcrumbs or Sao biscuit crumbs, or more as needed

1 teaspoon Worcestershire sauce

2 tablespoons cream

Remove oysters from shells and heat shells under a low griller.

Melt butter in a heavy frying pan, being careful not to let it burn. Add garlic, twist around pan for a few seconds for flavour, then discard. Add celery, red capsicum, freshly ground pepper and salt, and chopped bacon. Cook slowly until all is tender, 10 to 15 minutes. Add a pinch of cayenne.

Mix breadcrumbs with Worcestershire sauce and cream. Put aside.

Remove shells from under the hot griller, spoon a little celery, capsicum and bacon mixture into each shell, then place the fresh oyster on top.

Top with bread mixture and grill under medium heat until bread mixture is browned and oysters are just warmed through. If you think the oysters need more breadcrumbs, just sprinkle extra over.

Serves 2 to 4 as an entrée

Oyster Mornay Superb

Rich, succulent oysters in creamy white sauce. Who could ask for anything more?

2½ cups milk

1 small onion, finely chopped

freshly ground pepper

pinch salt

4 drops Tabasco sauce

pinch dried basil or dill

½ teaspoon celery salt

2 tablespoons plain flour

1 teaspoon mustard

1 tablespoon butter

1 large carrot, scraped and grated

2 tablespoons cream

24 beautiful oysters on the shell

tasty cheese, grated

Put milk to heat in a saucepan, add onion, pepper, salt, Tabasco sauce, basil and celery salt. Mix plain flour and mustard to a smooth paste with water.

When milk mixture is very hot, but not boiling, stir in flour and mustard mixture. Add butter, stir until all is combined and thickened. Cook slowly for 15 minutes, stirring occasionally to see that mixture does not stick and burn. When ready, stir in grated carrot; remove from stove and stir in cream.

Remove oysters from shell and add to sauce in saucepan. Return pan to stove to warm through. Meanwhile heat shells under a hot griller. When all is ready, fill shells with oysters and sauce, sprinkle with grated cheese and put under the griller again, to brown. Superb!

Serves 2 to 4 as an entrée

Devilled Oysters

2 tablespoons butter

2 teaspoons curry powder, or to taste

1 tablespoon Worcestershire sauce

1 teaspoon anchovy sauce

small pinch cayenne pepper

juice of 1 lemon

2 eggs, well beaten

1 cup milk

2 teaspoons cornflour (cornstarch)

24 oysters, bottled or on the shell

paprika

lemon wedges

Mix butter, curry powder, Worcestershire sauce, anchovy sauce, a tiny pinch of cayenne and lemon juice in a bowl. Add beaten eggs and milk and mix well.

Pour mixture into saucepan. Cook slowly for 10 minutes, stirring, then thicken with cornflour that has been mixed to a smooth paste with a little milk.

When mixture has boiled and thickened, add the oysters. Do not overcook the oysters; just cook for a few minutes to reheat and flavour.

Serve on a bed of fluffy rice, with a sprinkle of paprika and plenty of lemon wedges. If you like your oysters hotter, just increase the quantity of curry powder.

Serves 4 as an entrée, 2 as a main course

John Doyle's Oysters with Avocado and Crabmeat

2 to 3 dozen oysters, in their shells

100 g (3½ oz) butter

½ cup plain flour

½ cup mayonnaise

½ cup tomato purée

½ cup milk

1 teaspoon curry powder

1 avocado

1 cup crabmeat (canned, if fresh not available)

½ cup cream

tasty cheese, grated

paprika

Place oysters in their shells on an oven dish, such as a scone tray. Preheat oven to 180°C (350°F).

Melt butter, taking care not to let it burn, and add flour to make a roux. Add mayonnaise, tomato purée, milk and curry powder. Stir to make a smooth mixture, and cook slowly for 5 minutes. Allow to cool.

Mash avocado and crabmeat together; add to cooled mixture. Place mixture carefully on top of oysters, then add a little cream to each oyster. Place tasty cheese over the top, dust with paprika and bake for 10 minutes.

Serve on warm plates with toasted bread or thin, crustless brown bread and butter sandwiches, cut into quarters, or that never-to-be forgotten (day and night hiccups) garlic bread.

Serves 6

Baked Oysters Blue Vein

Janette Howard was kind enough to share with me the recipe for this fabulous dish.

4 dozen oysters on shell, or 1 bottle
    50 oysters, drained (6 oysters per head)
¼ cup sour light cream
½ teaspoon Tabasco sauce
3 tablespoons finely chopped fresh basil
1 tablespoon fresh lemon juice
1 tablespoon butter or margarine
1 cup fresh wholemeal breadcrumbs
2 cloves garlic, crushed
2 tablespoons blue vein cheese, grated
freshly ground black pepper

Preheat oven to 200°C (400°F).

Arrange opened oysters on an oven tray, or, if using bottled oysters, divide between 4 ovenproof dishes.

Combine sour cream, Tabasco sauce, basil and lemon juice in a bowl. Mix well.

Melt butter or margarine in a saucepan, add breadcrumbs and garlic, and stir until crisp and golden. Remove from heat and add blue vein cheese and pepper. Spoon the basil sour cream evenly over the oysters and top with the cheese and breadcrumb mixture.

Bake for 12 minutes.

Serves 8

Earle Clendanial's Oyster Omelette

This recipe comes from Earle Clendanial, Sarasota, Florida.

9 large eggs
⅔ cup dry breadcrumbs
3–4 dozen freshly shucked oysters, drained
¼ cup plain flour
6 slices of bacon
¼ teaspoon salt
¼ teaspoon lemon and pepper seasoning
1 heaped teaspoon fresh chopped chives
paprika, to garnish

In a small bowl, beat 1 egg. Spread half the breadcrumbs on waxed paper. Dip each oyster first in flour, then in egg and place in a single layer on breadcrumbs. Toss lightly to coat oysters well and set aside.

In a 30 cm (12 in) frying pan, fry bacon until crispy. Remove and drain. Place oysters in the frying pan in a single layer. Cook until oysters are golden brown on both sides, about 5 minutes.

In a medium bowl, beat the remaining eggs until foamy. Crumble bacon and add it to the eggs with the seasonings and chives. Pour mixture over oysters, sprinkle with remaining breadcrumbs and cook over low heat until mixture begins to set around the edges. With spatula, gently lift edges as they set, tilting the pan to allow uncooked egg mix to flow under the omelette. Cook until egg mixture is set but is still moist on the surface.

Add paprika, serve immediately and enjoy.

Serves 4 to 6

Mussels

Mussels are delicious and they're a really clean shellfish because all the dirt is on the outside and none penetrates inside. Don't be put off buying them because they are sold in the shell – they are easy to prepare and well worthwhile.

Preparing Mussels

Mussels need to be cleaned and de-bearded before cooking. Wash mussels under running water, and remove all traces of mud, seaweed and barnacles with a brush or knife; remove beards (the rough, furry part around the mussel). If mussel shells are cracked or broken, discard them. If any mussels are slightly open, tap sharply, and if they do not close, discard.

Steamed Mussels

3 tablespoons olive oil

2 tablespoons unsalted butter

2 cloves garlic, finely chopped

6 green onions (scallions), finely sliced

1 cup dry white wine

½ cup flat-leaf (Italian) parsley, chopped

48 black mussels, cleaned and de-bearded

½ cup pouring cream

Heat the olive oil and butter in a large saucepan and add the garlic and green onions. Stir for 2-3 minutes until aromatic.

Add the wine, parsley and mussels and stir. Cover and cook over a high heat, shaking the pan occasionally, for 3-5 minutes until the mussels open. Remove the mussels and discard any that do not open.

Add the cream to the remaining juices and stir over a medium heat for about 3 minutes.

Spoon the mussels into large soup bowls and pour over the cream sauce.

Serves 4

Mussels à la Portuguese

I don't know why we call this dish 'Portuguese' — we get the mussels in Sydney. In fact, in my day mussels were exclusive to us Watsons Bay locals. Anyway, it's a smart name and a dish cooked to perfection by my grandson Peter at Doyles on the Beach at Watsons Bay.

4 green onions (scallions), finely chopped

1 clove garlic, chopped

2 tablespoons olive oil

3 teaspoons butter

⅔ cup dry white wine

⅓ cup water

3 teaspoons finely chopped parsley

2 fresh thyme sprigs or pinch dried thyme

1 or 2 bay leaves

½ teaspoon ground black pepper

1-1.5 kg (2-3 lb) mussels, cleaned and de-bearded

½ cup fresh cream

extra chopped parsley

lemon quarters

Gently fry green onion and garlic in olive oil and butter until transparent but not coloured. Add wine, water, parsley, thyme, bay leaf, pepper and mussels. Pour cream over the top. Cover pan, bring to the boil and steam over a high heat for about 4 minutes, shaking pan constantly. The shells will open as the mussels cook.

Serve as soon as the shells open. Discard any that do not open.

Serve in deep bowls like mixing bowls, garnished with chopped parsley and lemon quarters. Mmmm – delicious.

Don't forget a large spoon to scoop up the juice.

Serves 2-3

Opposite: Young Doyles

Scallops

Scallops are refined, delicate, versatile and more-ish little shellfish – so smart and pretty when they are all cleaned up. There are so many different gourmet dishes that can be made with scallops. Once you know a little about them, cooking with them is, to quote my favourite saying, 'just a breeze' – like that beautiful nor'-easter that floats across Sydney Harbour on a hot summer's day. Very easy to take (the breeze and the scallops). Scallops can be tough if overcooked, so take care.

Scallops Mornay

2 large tablespoons butter or margarine

2 tablespoons plain flour

½ teaspoon dried dill

½ teaspoon dried basil

freshly ground pepper

½ teaspoon salt

4 drops Tabasco sauce

1 teaspoon Worcestershire sauce

3¾ cups milk, or half milk and half fish stock

2 bay leaves

sticks crisp celery, strings removed, chopped

1 small brown onion, grated

500 g (1 lb) scallops, from your friendly fish shop

1 carrot, peeled and grated

tasty cheese, grated

chopped parsley

paprika

lemon wedges

In a heavy saucepan, melt butter, add flour, stir until butter is absorbed into flour. Add dill, basil, pepper, salt, tabasco and Worcestershire sauces, then slowly add milk, stirring all the time until mixture boils and thickens.

Add unbroken bay leaves with celery and onion. Cook, stirring all the time for about 10 minutes, then turn heat very low.

Place scallops in another saucepan, just cover with water, bring to the boil then simmer for about 3 minutes.

Strain scallops and place them in the sauce with the grated carrot. Cook, stirring, for about 1 minute.

Pour mixture into individual ramekin bowls or a shallow ovenproof dish. Sprinkle grated cheese over and brown carefully under a hot griller.

Serve as an entrée or main course, garnished with finely chopped parsley, a sprinkle of paprika and lemon wedges. Brown or rye bread toasted and buttered while hot is nice on the side.

Serves 4

Breaded, Buttered Scallops

Rich but delicious — great served with crisp bacon and mushrooms.

plain flour, seasoned with salt and pepper

about 2 cups breadcrumbs or Sao biscuit crumbs

750 g (1½ lb) scallops

250 g (8 oz) bacon

1 egg

2 tablespoons cream

125 g (4 oz) butter

lemon slices

parsley sprigs

Place white butcher's paper on your workbench and spread with plain flour. Blend breadcrumbs or roll out biscuit crumbs.

Dry scallops. Cut rind off bacon and cut bacon in small pieces, cutting off as much fat as possible.

Mix egg and cream together in a bowl.

Toss scallops in flour, then in egg mixture and lastly in breadcrumbs.

Melt butter in a large, heavy pan, and when it is hot (do not burn), put in bacon and scallops and cook slowly for 10 minutes.

Serve on hot plates garnished with lemon and parsley.

Serves 4

Scallops and Mushrooms

Mushrooms seem to be at their best at the same time of the year as scallops, and luckily they go well together.

175 g (6 oz) butter

500 g (1 lb) small mushrooms, halved

½ bunch green onions (scallions), chopped

pepper and salt

750 g (1½ lb) scallops

1 small can tomatoes, drained

2 bay leaves

1 teaspoon sugar

pinch dried basil

1 clove garlic, crushed

2 sticks celery, chopped

4 drops Tabasco sauce

breadcrumbs

Preheat oven to 170°C (325°F).

Melt 125 g (4 oz) butter in pan. Place mushrooms and green onions in pan with some freshly ground pepper and salt, fry gently and put aside until needed.

Dry scallops and fry in remaining butter to which tomatoes have been added. Add bay leaves, sugar, basil, garlic, celery and Tabasco sauce. Cook all gently for 10 minutes.

Place mixture in a flat casserole dish, add mushrooms and mix well. Sprinkle with breadcrumbs and place in a warm oven until brown on top.

Serve with hot savoury bread or garlic bread.

Serves 4

Squid (Calamari)

I cannot get used to the name calamari, so I call it squid. Squid is naturally tough, to my mind, but it has a flavour all of its own. I've read so many complicated-sounding ways to cook squid that I'm going to leave you to sort those recipes out and just give you four of our ones – our son Tim's specialities.

Salt and Pepper Calamari

This dish is tasty served with sweet chilli sauce.

1½ tablespoons salt
1½ tablespoons finely ground pepper
8 medium calamari with tentacles,
   cleaned and sliced into 1 cm (½ in) rings
1½ cups cornflour (cornstarch)
vegetable oil for deep-frying
lemon wedges, for garnish

Combine the salt and pepper in a small pan and stir over medium heat for 3–5 minutes until light brown in colour. Remove and cool.

Sprinkle the salt and pepper mixture over the calamari rings and toss gently to coat. Then toss the calamari lightly in cornflour. Shake off any excess cornflour.

Deep-fry in hot oil for 3–5 minutes, or until tender and golden.

Drain and serve garnished with lemon wedges.

Serves 4

Deep-fried Calamari

1 kg (2 lb) squid, thoroughly cleaned and skinned
plain flour
pepper and salt
batter (see page 62)
olive oil for deep-frying
lemon wedges

Wash squid and pat dry. Cut into rings and toss in flour seasoned with salt and pepper.

Dip squid in batter and deep-fry carefully in hot oil for about 3 minutes until golden.

Serve hot with bread and lemon wedges.

Serves 4 to 6

Calamari with Wine, Tomato and Herbs

1 kg (2 lb) squid, thoroughly cleaned and skinned
1 cup olive oil
1 large clove garlic, crushed
salt and pepper
1½ teaspoons dried mixed dill and basil or oregano
1 cup Sauternes style wine
500 g (1 lb) ripe tomatoes or 1 can tomatoes, drained
2 teaspoons chopped parsley
small squares bread fried in olive oil for croutons

Wash squid, pat dry and cut into rings.

Heat oil in a heavy frying pan or saucepan, add garlic and cook for about 2 minutes. Then discard the garlic, otherwise it will mask the real flavour of the squid.

Fry squid in the oil for about 3 minutes or until opaque. Season with salt and pepper (freshly ground for better flavour), add herbs and cook slowly for another 3 minutes.

Add Sauternes, tomatoes and parsley, put lid on pan and simmer for a further 4 minutes.

Have warm plates ready and serve squid with fried bread croutons.

Serves 4-6

Garlic Squid

This is a quick and easy recipe.

4 tablespoons butter
4 garlic cloves, flattened and crushed
1 chilli, seeded and chopped
3 tablespoons chopped parsley
600 g (20 oz) prepared, cleaned calamari
   (available at most fish outlets), cut in rings

Heat butter in pan. Add garlic, chilli and half the parsley, stirring.

Add calamari, toss till coated. Stir for 4 minutes.

Serve topped with remaining parsley.

Serves 4 as an entrée

Octopus

Barbecued Octopus

Though octopus come in varying sizes, small octopus is most suitable for this recipe. Look for firm, resilient flesh and a fresh sea smell when you buy your octopus. Marinate overnight for the best flavour.

1 cup extra-virgin olive oil

1 cup lemon juice

4 cloves garlic, finely chopped

cracked black pepper to taste

1 kg (2 lb) baby octopus, cleaned with heads removed

lemon wedges

To make the marinade, combine the olive oil, lemon juice, garlic and pepper in a large saucepan and bring to the boil. Add the octopus and boil uncovered for 2–3 minutes. Remove and cool. Refrigerate the marinating octopus for at least 6 hours or overnight.

Remove the octopus from the marinade and cook on a hot barbecue or chargrill plate for 5–10 minutes, or until tender.

Serve with steamed rice and garnish with lemon wedges.

Serves 4

Seafood Extravaganzas

There are certain seafood dishes that are made with all kinds of different goodies – perfect for those seafood lovers who just can't decide what to choose from the menu. These dishes are really extra special, which is why they've got a section all to themselves. The good news, too, is that you can vary the ingredients to your heart's content, depending on what you like, how much of an impact you want to make on your guests and, of course, what's available in the fish markets at the time.

Tim Doyle's Avocado Seafood with Macadamia Nuts

A big favourite with Tim's customers at the Quay Restaurant, this delicious entrée is truly a luxury meal — but there are times when seafoods are more plentiful, and you may even live near the waterfront and be able to catch your own. While this seafood version is one for a special celebration, you can also use firm cooked fish with the bones removed.

350 ml (½ pint) French dressing (recipe page 146)

2 tablespoons honey, warmed

2 tablespoons lemon juice

salt and pepper

1 cup chopped macadamia nuts

2 large ripe but firm avocados

lobster pieces, cooked

flesh from Balmain bugs, cooked

prawn meat, cooked

lightly poached scallops (or substitute boned, firm cooked fish)

Mix together French dressing, warmed honey, lemon juice, and salt and pepper to taste. When well mixed, add chopped nuts.

Remove skin from avocados and chop flesh into bite-sized pieces. Combine in a bowl with seafoods and dressing mixture and refrigerate until ready to serve.

Arrange decoratively in deep, attractive bowls. Serve with hot, crusty bread rolls or garlic bread.

Serves 4

Doyles Paella

As served at Doyles on the Beach, Watsons Bay. I am not really giving away trade secrets, as the only secret of seafood cooking is fresh seafood.

50 g (1½ oz) squid, cleaned and cut into rings

¼ cup Spanish olive oil

1 tomato, peeled, seeded and chopped

2 tablespoons tomato paste

½ brown onion, chopped

1 clove garlic, finely chopped

2-3 bay leaves

50 g (1½ oz) green prawns, shelled

1½ kg (3 lb) green mud crab, cut in 3 pieces

3 or 4 mussels, cleaned

200 g (7 oz) fillets whitefish, cut in pieces

¼ cup water

¾ cup dry white wine

½ teaspoon paprika

salt and freshly ground pepper

3 cups cooked rice

saffron or paprika

finely chopped parsley

As large squid can take a long while to cook, I suggest you boil it first for an hour.

In a deep serving/cooking saucepan, heat the oil, add tomato, tomato paste, onion, garlic and bay leaves, stir well and add prawns, crab pieces, squid, mussels (see page 131 for preparation of mussels), and fish. Stir all again, then add water, wine, paprika, and salt and pepper and stir. Cook slowly for 10 minutes after the ingredients have come to the boil.

Serve in the pot you cooked it in.

Serve with a dish of hot fluffy rice sprinkled with saffron or paprika and finely chopped parsley.

Serves 2

To make garlic bread, take a stick of French bread and split it down the centre, butter heavily and spread with chopped garlic, damp all over with milk and place in a very hot oven. Decrease heat, warm through and serve. For a change, I like to brush the top of the bread with melted butter and sprinkle it with salad herbs.

Seafood Omelette

I never make an omelette until the person is seated at the table, because omelettes start to toughen from the moment they are cooked. An observation that I have made over the years in the restaurant is that, on receiving their omelette, most people will immediately cut it across the middle, gaze at it for a moment, and then start eating from the end. Why? I know not, but it's a fact!

3 eggs

salt and pepper to taste

butter

parsley, finely chopped or fried

Suggested Fillings

(choose your own combinations; choice is unlimited)

crab

lobster

salmon

fish of all kinds

oysters

One of the most easily prepared and succulent dishes, and in many cases the cheapest, is the omelette. Suitable for breakfast, luncheon, dinner or supper.

Mix eggs with salt and pepper and stir about 8 times with a fork. Do not beat or whip.

In a black iron or omelette pan, melt a knob of butter until it gives off a nutty smell. Then add your egg mixture, making sure that it covers the pan. Let it cook for about 12 to 15 seconds on good heat, then tilt the pan downwards and push forward with a thin-bladed pallet knife.

Do this several times with a rocking motion until the egg mixture is cooked. If it is a little wet, it does not matter, as the contained heat and filling will finish cooking it.

Hold the pan firmly in your hand and tap your wrist firmly. If the pan is well greased, the omelette will immediately slide forward until it starts to curl down. 'Tis then that you place your filling in. Give it a further few taps to complete the fold and slide it onto a heated plate.

Brush a little melted butter over it and garnish with parsley.

Serve with vegetables of your choice; green minted peas and julienne carrots make an attractive dish. With gourmet foods such as lobster, oysters, and so on, the addition of a tablespoon of béchamel or basic white sauce (recipes pages 150 and 149) to the filling will not spoil the omelette and will make the mixture go much further.

Serves 1

Pasta Marinara

500 g (1 lb) spaghetti

4 tablespoons extra-virgin olive oil

16 large green (raw) king prawns,
   shelled and de-veined with tails intact

extra basil and parsley leaves for garnish

Marinara Sauce

¼ cup extra-virgin olive oil

1 small onion, finely chopped

1 leek, finely chopped

2 cloves garlic, finely chopped

1 sprig flat-leaf (Italian) parsley

6 large basil leaves, chopped

4 sprigs fresh thyme

2 sprigs fresh rosemary

salt and pepper to taste

2 x 400 g (14 oz) cans tomatoes

1 cup dry red wine

2 tablespoons tomato paste

To make the marinara sauce, heat 3 tablespoons of olive oil in a medium-sized saucepan. Add the onion, leek and garlic and stir over medium heat for 2–3 minutes. Add the parsley, basil, thyme, rosemary, salt and pepper and stir to combine. Add the canned tomatoes (in their juice), red wine and tomato paste and stir to break up the tomatoes. Cover and simmer for 30 minutes, stirring occasionally.

Cook the spaghetti in a large saucepan of lightly salted boiling water until al dente. Drain.

Heat 4 tablespoons of olive oil in a large frying pan and sauté the prawns until they just change colour. This may need to be done in batches, depending on the size of the prawns.

Remove the parsley, thyme and rosemary from the marinara sauce and discard. Add the prawns to the sauce and stir to coat the prawns.

To serve, spoon the hot sauce over the spaghetti and garnish with extra basil and parsley leaves.

Serves 4

Thai-style Seafood Salad

Lobster, mud crab and spanner crab may be substituted for the blue swimmer crab and Balmain bugs in this recipe.

Sugar Syrup Dressing

1½ cups caster (superfine) sugar

¾ cup water

½ cup white vinegar

4 tablespoons lime juice

¼ cup fresh coriander (cilantro), chopped

2 small red chillies, seeds
    removed and finely chopped (or to taste)

1 teaspoon finely chopped fresh ginger

1 clove garlic, finely chopped

cracked black pepper to taste

Salad

1–2 heads baby cos lettuce

½ cup fresh coriander (cilantro) leaves

20 medium-sized basil leaves

½ cup fresh chervil leaves

2 cups small fresh sorrel leaves

8 cooked king prawns, peeled, with tails intact

2 cooked blue swimmer crabs, meat removed

4 cooked Balmain bugs, meat removed and halved

1 red capsicum, seeded and finely sliced

To make the dressing, combine the sugar and water in a medium saucepan and stir over low heat until the sugar is dissolved. Remove from the heat and cool. Pour 180 ml (¾ cup) of the sugar syrup into a bowl, then add the vinegar and lime juice and whisk until well combined. Add the remaining dressing ingredients and mix well.

To make the salad, combine the lettuce, coriander, basil, chervil and sorrel leaves in a large bowl, cover and refrigerate for about 15 minutes or until crisp. Add the prawns, crabmeat and bug meat and 3 tablespoons (¼ cup) of the dressing, then toss gently to combine.

Arrange the seafood salad on serving plates and pour over the remaining dressing.

Garnish with red capsicum.

Serves 4

Warm Salad of Pan-fried Seafood

Salad

1½ tablespoons olive oil

8 green (raw) king prawns,
    peeled and de-veined with tails intact

8 Queensland scallops, well drained

12 strips cuttlefish (about 10 cm x 1 cm/5 in x ½ in)

cracked black pepper to taste

2 tablespoons lemon juice

2 heads baby cos lettuce leaves, torn

1 bunch sorrel leaves

1 small red capsicum, finely sliced

Dressing

2½ tablespoons extra-virgin olive oil

2½ tablespoons lemon juice

1 clove garlic, finely chopped

cracked black pepper

sea salt

To prepare the salad, heat the olive oil in a large, heavy-based frying pan. Add the prawns, scallops and cuttlefish. Stir over a high heat until the seafood is just cooked. Add the pepper and lemon juice and stir to combine.

Remove from the heat and combine the seafood in a large bowl (reserving the juices) with torn lettuce leaves, sorrel and capsicum.

Place all the dressing ingredients in a screw-top jar and shake well to combine.

Pour the dressing over the salad and toss gently to combine.

Arrange the salad on serving plates and pour remaining seafood juices over the top of each serving.

Top with extra cracked black pepper.

Serves 4

Peking Firepot

This recipe was given to me by John Singleton, who describes it as a sort of seafood fondue gone wrong! It's quite a lot of work, but well worth the effort. John says that the best thing about it all is that if you are really hungry you can go on for hours and, even when it's finished, the bits and pieces that have fallen into the stock — the noodles, cabbage, and so on — make a really good soup. And if you are not hungry, it is easy to look as if you are enjoying it without really eating anything much!

1 fresh cuttlefish

500 g (1 lb) fillets of firm fish

500 g (1 lb) scallops

500 g (1 lb) green (raw) prawns, shelled and de-veined

2 green lobster tails

3 dozen oysters

4 large crab claws

dry white wine

2 cloves garlic, finely chopped

10 cups fish or chicken stock, heated

125 g (4 oz) fine noodles

1 kg (2 lb) fresh bean sprouts

1 dozen leaves won bok (Chinese lettuce)

1 bunch bok choy (Chinese cabbage)

3 dozen fish balls (recipe below)

2 large carrots, thinly sliced

3 zucchini

8 cups hot cooked brown rice (1 cup per person)

8 lettuce leaves

8 eggs

Fish Balls

500 g (1 lb) fish fillets

250 g (8 oz) green (raw) prawns, shelled and de-veined

30 g (1 oz) pork fat

1 slice ham (optional)

parsley

salt

1 tablespoon white wine

1 tablespoon cornflour (cornstarch)

1 egg white, lightly beaten

won ton skins (optional)

Equipment for Serving

1 large or 2 small fondue pots

Chinese soup baskets

chopsticks or fondue forks

variety of sauces – soy, chilli, hoi sin and so on

Cut fish and shellfish into bite-sized pieces. Marinate fish fillets and scallops separately in a little white wine and finely chopped garlic. When it is time to eat, arrange fish and shellfish in individual serving dishes.

Make the fish balls ahead of time by mincing together fish, prawns, pork fat, ham and parsley, then pounding until smooth. Season with salt and wine, add cornflour and egg white, then leave to stand for 1 hour until firm. Form into walnut-sized balls or, alternatively, make won tons. (Put a little fish mixture in centre of won ton pastry square, wet two edges and fold over to make triangle, then wet two corners and press tightly together to form ear-shaped won ton.)

Heat stock to boiling point in fondue dish, and add noodles, bean sprouts, won bok, bok choy, fish balls, carrot pieces and zucchinis. Guests take pieces of fish, dip in boiling stock for 1 minute, then into a sauce, in usual fondue fashion, and help themselves to food already in the pot. You can use fondue forks or chopsticks. (Chopsticks are much more fun – and much more messy.) Each person should have a bowlful of rice to catch the drips.

When the bite-sized pieces are gone, drop a lettuce leaf cup into the stock, break an egg into it and poach.

Serves 8

Seafood in a White Peppercorn Sauce

For this delicious recipe, my thanks go to Dr Lola Power.

1 kg (2 lb) cooked prawns, shelled

750 g (1½ lb) pearl perch fillets, boned and skinned

2 tablespoons butter

1 tablespoon plain flour

1 small white onion, grated

1 teaspoon dry mustard

1 small leaf fresh basil, chopped

1 bay leaf, crumbled

½ teaspoon dill

1 cup milk

300 ml (10 fl oz) cream

salt

1 teaspoon tinned green peppercorns, pounded

1 egg, beaten

1 carrot, grated

1 large stalk celery, chopped

1 small brown onion, roughly chopped

500 g (1 lb) button mushrooms, sliced

dash Tabasco sauce (optional)

Parmesan cheese

parsley

paprika

Preheat oven to 220°C (425°F).

Chop prawns and cut fish in small portions. Put aside.

Melt butter in saucepan, and when hot add flour, stirring until smooth and mixture leaves sides of saucepan. Turn heat down, add grated onion, mustard, basil, bay leaf and dill.

Gradually add milk, stirring all the time until sauce is smooth.

Add cream, still stirring; add salt and pounded green peppercorns. Stir egg in carefully, add grated carrot. Do not allow sauce to boil after egg is added.

In a separate pan cook fish for 5 minutes in a little water to which celery, salt and brown onion have been added. Drain and try not to let fish break up. Mix prawns and fish gently with sauce and warm through.

Place sliced mushrooms in the bottom of a heated casserole, then carefully spoon in sauce and fish mixture. Test sauce for flavour, adding Tabasco, salt, or other seasonings if required. Grate a little Parmesan cheese on top, place in a hot oven for a few minutes to brown. Decorate with chopped parsley and a sprinkle of paprika.

Serve immediately with vegetables such as hot asparagus, creamed celery, potatoes chipped and fried in butter, or zucchini, heated soft bread rolls and a dish of scooped-out lemon pulp as well as lemon wedges.

Serves 6

Dressings, Sauces

& Stuffings

Dressings & Cold Sauces

The well-chosen stuffing or sauce — either hot or cold — can turn simply cooked fish or seafood into a gourmet meal. When you are deciding on a special dinner for friends and family, don't forget this. What could be nicer than freshly cooked, piping hot grilled fish with a prawn or anchovy sauce; humble fried fish with homemade tartare sauce; or freshly caught trout with the perfect stuffing?

Thick fish fillets or steaks should always be served with a sauce, as they tend to be dry. A good sauce can be easily made by cooking tomatoes, onion and celery together with a few herbs and seasoning to taste; or follow one of the recipes in this chapter. Serve the sauce in a separate jug or bowl, then everyone can have as much as he or she wants.

You will find the cocktail sauce useful, too, for when you have prawns at home.

Classic Mayonnaise

This is a superb dressing and well worth the effort.

1 cup olive or polyunsaturated oil (olive oil is best)

2 egg yolks

1 teaspoon mustard, made with mustard powder

1 teaspoon salt

½ teaspoon cayenne pepper

1 teaspoon caster sugar (or ordinary sugar)

2 dashes Tabasco sauce

2 teaspoons vinegar

2 teaspoons tarragon vinegar

2 teaspoons lemon juice

You can add to this basic mayonnaise anything you choose. If your mixture curdles before you add the vinegars, and so on, drop by drop add the beaten yolk of one more egg.

Put the oil in a jug. Put aside.

Using a wooden spoon, mix egg yolks, mustard, salt, cayenne pepper, sugar and Tabasco sauce. Stir it around until you think it looks a bit 'queer'. Don't worry, keep stirring. While stirring, slowly add the oil drop by drop. (If you add the oil too quickly, your mixture will curdle.) As you add the oil, you will notice it gets thicker and richer.

When all the oil is absorbed and you have a smooth coating consistency, add the vinegars slowly and then slowly add the lemon juice.

Makes about 1 cup

Easy Egg Yolk Dressing

I like tarragon vinegar best in this dressing.

2 egg yolks

1 teaspoon mustard

1 teaspoon caster sugar or ordinary sugar

freshly ground pepper

salt

300 ml (10 fl oz) fresh cream

vinegar, brown or white

dash paprika

Mix egg yolks, mustard, sugar, pepper and salt with some of the cream to a smooth consistency. Add vinegar to taste, then carefully add more cream until you reach the desired consistency. The mixture will thicken as it stands. Add paprika.

Be careful of curdling when making this dressing. If the mixture does curdle, beat in another egg yolk, then add a little more cream.

Avocado Dressing

A favourite with our customers, this is a perfect dressing for side salads. Some like it for fish as well.
You can use it with any meat dish or salad, or have it on the side as a sauce. I make it in my food processor.

Keep this dressing in the fridge, but make sure it doesn't get too cold as the oil will separate from the other ingredients.

2 cloves garlic, crushed

1 teaspoon sugar

1 teaspoon dry mustard

1 teaspoon salad herbs

½ teaspoon dry dill (optional)

salt and pepper

3 drops Tabasco sauce

1 small green capsicum

1 small red capsicum (with seeds)

2 sticks celery

2 large avocados

2 cups salad oil (olive oil is good)

⅓ cup tarragon vinegar

2 teaspoons malt vinegar

Blend together garlic, sugar, mustard, salad herbs, dill, salt, pepper and Tabasco sauce. Add chopped capsicums and celery. Add flesh of avocados. Blend thoroughly for a few seconds. Add half the oil and vinegar while machine is running, then add the rest of the oil and vinegar together.

Carefully pour into jars and shake occasionally to distribute the mixture evenly.

French Dressing

If you like a sweeter dressing, add 1 teaspoon caster sugar.

This is about the most popular dressing for avocados. I make it in a large jar which has a tight–fitting plastic lid. It can also be made in a cocktail shaker which has measurements.

1 cup olive or salad oil

⅓ cup tarragon or brown vinegar

1 clove garlic, bruised

1 teaspoon salad herbs

½ teaspoon paprika

freshly ground pepper

salt

Put all ingredients into your shaker, blender or jar and shake vigorously. Chill. Remove the garlic when ready to use. Shake each time you use it.

Spicy Dressing

This dressing is perfect to serve with avocados.

2 tablespoons fresh, good-quality tomato sauce

1 teaspoon French mustard

1 tablespoon horseradish sauce

1 teaspoon Worcestershire sauce

juice of 1 large lemon

pinch salt

Beat all ingredients together and use whenever needed.

Enough to dress two halves of an avocado

Egg Sauce with Chives

A tasty addition to grilled, baked or fried fish.

3 eggs, hard-boiled, cold

2 or 3 tablespoons olive oil

½ teaspoon salt

1 tablespoon brown vinegar

1 teaspoon sugar

2 tablespoons chopped chives

Peel eggs and cut them in halves. Sieve the yolks and chop the whites finely. Mix with olive oil and salt, then add vinegar, sugar and chives.

Epicurean Sauce

A can of drained asparagus added to this sauce makes it extra special.

gelatine to make ¼ cup aspic jelly

1 cucumber

1 tablespoon tarragon vinegar

½ cup mayonnaise

¼ cup cream

1 teaspoon anchovy essence

2 teaspoons gherkins, chopped

2 teaspoons chutney, chopped

sugar, to taste

salt and pepper, to taste

Make aspic jelly by dissolving 2 teaspoons gelatine in ½ cup warm water. Let stand, but don't allow it to go too cold.

Peel cucumber, cut into small pieces and cook until tender in salted water. Drain off water and rub cucumber through a sieve.

Mix cucumber purée with vinegar and aspic, which should be just lukewarm. Carefully mix mayonnaise with cream, anchovy essence, gherkins and chutney.

Blend both mixtures together. Season with sugar, salt and pepper and serve.

Cocktail Sauce

This tasty, easy-to-make recipe is great for seafood dips and entrees. It is also excellent with fried prawns and oysters, and it even goes well with meat pies, frankfurts, sausage rolls and chips!

½ cup mayonnaise

6 tablespoons tomato sauce

½ small can reduced cream

2 teaspoons Worcestershire sauce

1 tablespoon brown vinegar or lemon

1 teaspoon horseradish sauce

freshly ground pepper

salt

pinch basil

parsley, finely chopped

dash Tabasco sauce

Add crushed garlic if desired. Also, add some extra tomato sauce for foods like chips and pies — this makes the sauce go further.

Shake all ingredients thoroughly, or mix in a blender. Serve.

Tartare Sauce

Tartare sauce in my opinion is used with seafoods far more than any other sauce.
Here is a popular recipe which is easy to make.

2 cups mayonnaise

1 white onion, chopped

6 gherkins, chopped

1 stalk celery, finely chopped

1 teaspoon capers, chopped

1 teaspoon parsley, finely chopped

1 clove garlic, crushed and minced finely

1 tablespoon chives, chopped

1 teaspoon tarragon vinegar

1 teaspoon red pimento (pepper)

dash of Tabasco sauce

salt and pepper

To make a successful tartare sauce, the ingredients must be chopped very finely. You can use a blender for this if you wish.

Combine all ingredients. Bottle and store in the refrigerator. Use when needed with all seafoods.

For variations on this sauce, add stuffed olives or well-drained finely chopped spinach — this will make the sauce a green colour. Some people use artificial colouring in tartare sauce, but I think it is better to use vegetable juices.

Grandfather's Favourite Fish Sauce

This simple sauce is delicious to serve with fried fish and chips. Sure to become a family favourite!

4 cups malt vinegar

2 tablespoons soy sauce

3 green onions (scallions), sliced

1 clove garlic

2 tablespoons walnut ketchup

3 drops Tabasco sauce or pinch cayenne pepper

Place all ingredients in a large bottle and shake vigorously.

Date the bottle and put it in a cupboard. Shake every day for two weeks. Then divide into smaller bottles and store until ready to use.

Walnut ketchup is obtainable at large delicatessens, or you can make it yourself when green walnuts are in season. Pickled walnuts may be substituted for the ketchup.

Walnut pickle or sauce may be unobtainable in your area, but you can make it yourself when green walnuts are in season.

Shaka Sauce

This sauce can be made only by stay-at-home cooks, as it needs to be shaken 2 or 3 times a day, for a month!

4 cups malt vinegar

2 cloves garlic, finely chopped

4 tablespoons walnut pickle or sauce

2½ tablespoons soy sauce

2½ tablespoons mushroom stir-fry sauce

1½ tablespoons mango pickle

Place all ingredients in a large, well-corked bottle and shake vigorously.

Date the bottle and put it in a cupboard. Shake 2 or 3 times daily (put the alarm on to remind you). At the end of a month this sauce will be ready to use.

Leghorn Sauce

This is an old-fashioned sauce for cold fish dishes and also for hot fillets of fish.

3 egg yolks, hard-boiled

vegetable oil or olive oil

3 anchovies, pounded or chopped

tarragon vinegar to taste

½ teaspoon parsley, finely chopped

nutmeg to taste

pepper to taste

Crush egg yolks with a wooden spoon. Add oil, drop by drop at first, until the mixture is the consistency of thick cream. Stir in the rest of the ingredients. Refrigerate until required.

Maître d'Hôtel Butter

60 g (2 oz) butter, softened

1 teaspoon parsley, finely chopped

1 teaspoon lemon juice

salt and pepper to taste

Mix all ingredients well. Spread on a plate and refrigerate. Use when required. Delicious on grilled or steamed fish.

Anchovy Butter

This is a tasty savoury spread or topping on grilled fish.

125 g (4 oz) butter

½ teaspoon anchovy essence or paste

pinch cayenne pepper

few drops cochineal or carmine

Mix all ingredients well. Be careful when adding colouring.

This makes only a small amount of spread, enough for a few biscuits or 2 serves of fish.

Hot Sauces

Clarified Butter

Sometimes called oiled or melted butter or ghee, clarified butter is often served instead of sauce with meat, fish and vegetables. It can also be used to moisten the surface of grilled food or dishes cooked au gratin. It gives excellent results when used for cooking instead of whole butter.

Place butter in a small pan. Let it heat slowly, removing the scum as it rises. When the butter looks like clear salad oil, carefully pour it into a container, leaving the sediment at the bottom of the pan. Serve hot.

Butter Sauce

Credit for this sauce goes to George Heydon, who once said: 'My father used to tell me of a Murray Cod that was so big that it had to back up twice to get around the bend in the river.' That really is a 'big fish' yarn, George.

125 g (4 oz) butter

grated nutmeg

pinch each dried dill and basil

freshly ground pepper

salt

2 tablespoons plain flour

2 cups milk

juice of 1 lemon

Put butter and seasonings in a saucepan. Stir in flour. Add milk, stirring all the time, and simmer gently. Add lemon juice. Do not allow to boil. Serve immediately.

Vegetable Sauce

My sister Flo's recipe for a sauce to go with her Old-fashioned Rissoles (recipe page 72). Without the addition of cream (see note in margin), this is an excellent fat-free sauce for grilled or steamed fish.

1 small can tomatoes

1 onion, sliced and chopped

1 clove garlic, crushed (optional)

1 stick celery, chopped

½ red pepper, chopped

1 teaspoon sugar

pinch basil

salt and pepper

Put everything in a saucepan and boil rapidly until the juice of the tomatoes is reduced and the sauce is concentrated and thick.

Thickened cream added to this sauce makes it really super. Also, a tablespoon of chutney is another variation. Chutney added later puts this into the upper-class bracket!

Foundation White Sauce

This is a smooth sauce for fish and shellfish. I often add to this basic sauce my favourite herbs and seasonings. Add chopped parsley to make parsley sauce; 2 cups of grated cheese and a dash of ready-made mustard to make cheese sauce; or for something different add a finely chopped celery stalk and a grated carrot.

1½ tablespoons butter or margarine

2 tablespoons plain flour

2 cups fish stock (recipe page 41)
    or milk, or a combination of both

freshly ground pepper

salt

dash of Tabasco sauce

herbs or seasonings of choice

Place butter or margarine in a saucepan over a low flame and melt. Add flour and cook carefully for a few minutes, stirring, making sure no lumps form. Stir constantly to avoid burning or browning. Gradually stir in the fish stock or milk. Add the seasonings.

Boil gently for about 10 minutes until smooth and thick.

Foundation white sauce with all its variations can be made in advance and reheated when ready to serve.

When using this sauce for oysters, add a little Worcestershire sauce to taste.

Béchamel Sauce

This sauce should be very smooth. Work on it — you will master it in the end!

2 cups milk, or half milk and half fish stock
   (recipe page 41)

5 peppercorns

½ blade mace or pinch powdered mace

1 small bay leaf

½ teaspoon dried herbs or a few sprigs fresh herbs

salt to taste

white roux paste made with 1 tablespoon melted butter
   with 1 tablespoon plain flour

pepper

dash Tabasco sauce

Heat milk (or milk and fish stock) in a saucepan with peppercorns, mace, bay leaf, herbs and salt. Simmer for about 15 minutes. Strain the seasonings from the milk.

Make the roux in a clean pan. Add the strained milk, stirring all the time. Boil gently for about 10 minutes. Season with pepper and salt and a dash of Tabasco sauce.

Pass this sauce through a fine strainer.

Anchovy Sauce

Here's a tasty accompaniment for grilled fish that is quick to make.

3 anchovies (soaked overnight in water)

½ onion, finely chopped

parsley, finely chopped

2 tablespoons flour

1 tablespoon butter

water

salt (optional)

Clean the soaked anchovies and chop finely. Discard soaking water. Add onion and parsley. Brown the flour in the butter, stirring, and then add anchovies and cook for only 1 minute.

Add water slowly, stirring, until required thickness is reached, then cook carefully for 15 minutes.

Taste sauce before adding salt because anchovies are very salty. A good way of reducing the saltiness of anchovies is to soak them in milk for 20 to 30 minutes before using.

Sweet and Sour Sauce

This sauce is the ideal dressing for Pacific Platter (recipe page 76).

125 g (4 oz) can pineapple pieces, including liquid

2 stalks celery, strings removed, chopped

1 onion, sliced or cut in squares

1 carrot, sliced

½ red or green capsicum, chopped into strips or squares

1 cup water

2 pieces ginger in syrup, or ginger root, finely chopped

2 teaspoons golden syrup

1 tablespoon brown vinegar

juice from 1 medium-sized can tomatoes

dash Tabasco sauce

1 dessertspoon arrowroot

Put all ingredients except arrowroot in saucepan and cook slowly for 10 minutes. Dissolve arrowroot in a small quantity of water and thicken sauce with this, stirring for a few minutes until arrowroot is cooked.

Care must be taken not to cook vegetables until soft; they should retain some crispness.

Caper Sauce

A delicious, smooth sauce for all fish dishes.

1 tablespoon butter or margarine

2 tablespoons flour

about 1 cup fish stock (recipe page 41), boiling hot

2 tablespoons capers, chopped

liquid from capers

salt

freshly ground pepper

1 tablespoon cream

1 egg yolk (optional)

Melt butter or margarine in a deep saucepan, taking care it does not burn. Stir in the flour carefully. This will go into a ball. To mix to a smooth paste, gradually add the fish stock.

Add the chopped capers and a little of the liquid from the capers bottle and cook for about 10 minutes. Season with salt and pepper to taste. Stir constantly to get rid of any lumps of flour.

When the sauce is just about cooked, stir in cream. If you want to be lavish, also stir in an egg yolk.

Ye Olde-fashioned Prawn Sauce

Serve over fish casseroles, or grilled or steamed fish. You'll get plenty of praise for this one.

500 g (1 lb) cooked school prawns, peeled

1 cup foundation white sauce (recipe page 149)

½ teaspoon anchovy essence

cayenne pepper, to taste

few drops lemon juice

Use the shells and heads of the prawns to make the stock you will need for the foundation white sauce.

To heated white sauce add the prawns, anchovy essence, cayenne pepper and lemon juice. Cover the saucepan and let sauce cook on a low flame without boiling for a few minutes. Serve hot.

Pacific Sea Sauce

250 g (8 oz) tomato sauce

¼ cup chopped chilli

1 teaspoon sugar

1 teaspoon Worcestershire sauce

¼ teaspoon garlic powder

¼ teaspoon ground oregano

¼ teaspoon dried thyme

a few leaves of basil

Combine all ingredients in a saucepan. Simmer for 10 to 12 minutes, stirring occasionally.

Makes about 1 large cup

Curry Sauce

Serve this sauce on top of Pacific Platter (recipe page 76) or with baked, fried, steamed or grilled fish.

2 tablespoons butter or margarine

1 large brown onion, chopped

2 sticks celery, strings removed, chopped

1 medium-sized can of tomatoes

500 g (1 lb) ripe tomatoes

1 small capsicum or ½ large capsicum

garlic, crushed

2 teaspoons curry powder (or to taste)

2 bay leaves, crushed

½ teaspoon dried basil

½ teaspoon pepper

½ teaspoon salt

2 teaspoons sugar

grated rind of 1 lemon

juice of 1 lemon

dash Tabasco sauce

juice from canned tomatoes or water

In a large frying pan, melt butter and brown onion (do not burn) and cook slowly. Add celery, drained canned tomatoes (reserve liquid), chopped fresh tomatoes, capsicum, garlic, curry powder, bay leaves, basil, pepper and salt.

Cook for 10 minutes over a medium heat. Add sugar, lemon, Tabasco sauce and tomato juice or water to make quantity and thickness required. Heat through.

You can add extra vegetables to this sauce, if you like. Cream can be added as well, and instead of water you can use white wine.

Hollandaise Sauce

I am especially partial to this sauce. It is rather rich, and I always add some of my favourite herbs to dress it up.

1 to 4 egg yolks, depending on quantity of sauce required

milk or fish stock (recipe page 41)

1 cup foundation white sauce or béchamel sauce (recipe page 149 or 150)

lemon juice

cayenne pepper

salt

pinch dried basil or nutmeg

Heat your sauce slowly.

Beat the egg yolks with a little milk or stock. (If you are making a large quantity of sauce, add each yolk separately.) Add to the sauce and stir over a low flame until cooked and thick. Add lemon juice, cayenne, salt, and basil or nutmeg.

If you think the sauce is too thick, add more stock or milk to make the consistency required.

Sometimes I add a small amount of mustard or a dash or two of Tabasco sauce to my hollandaise.

Roux Paste

Roux is the French name for a paste used for thickening sauces, soups and gravies. The roux may be white or brown, depending on how long it is cooked. White roux is used for white sauces. Roux paste is a rich foundation for any sauce.

Take equal quantities of butter and plain flour.

Melt butter, stir in flour. Cook, stirring, for a few minutes without browning.

If a blond or brown roux is required, cook for a little longer until colour deepens.

Tasty Sauce for Smoked Fish

This sauce is another George Heydon speciality.

roux paste (instructions above)

milk in which smoked fish has been poached

seasoning to taste

hard-boiled eggs, chopped

cucumber, chopped

Make a roux paste, using plain flour or cornflour. Add milk and seasoning to taste, then eggs and cucumber.

Pour the sauce over the fish, and serve.

Stuffings

Stuffing for Fish 1

Stuff the inside of a fish with this and sew up the opening.
This stuffing is suitable for smaller fish, which cook quickly.

½ cup breadcrumbs

60 g (2 oz) butter

2 anchovies, canned (optional), or salt to taste

6 tablespoons cream or milk

2 egg yolks

1 dozen oysters, chopped

Blend or thoroughly mix breadcrumbs, butter and
anchovies. Add the cream or milk and the egg yolks.

Put the mixture in a saucepan and heat and stir the
mixture until it thickens, which should take about
5 minutes. Remove from heat. Add oysters and mix well.

Stuffing for Fish 2

Here is another stuffing for good measure. After all, that
large fish Dad caught or won in a raffle deserves the best.
The mixture can be used as a filling for a whole fish or it
can be served on top of baked fillets of fish, when it should
be placed over the fish 10 minutes before the end of the
cooking time.

60 g (2 oz) butter

1 tablespoon plain flour

1 cup milk or fish stock (recipe page 41)

2 eggs

salt and pepper

500 g (1 lb) boned, chopped raw fish
(cod, salmon, gemfish are ideal)

Melt butter, stir in flour, add milk or fish stock and cook
until mixture is a compact mass around the bowl of the
spoon. Add eggs one by one, beat in well. Season well with
salt and pepper, then pass mixture through a wire sieve.

Add chopped fish, and mix well.

A lighter mixture can be obtained when required by
blending or pounding 3 egg yolks with the fish and mixing
in 3 egg whites, whipped until they are stiff. Do this after
passing the mixture through a sieve.

Slaking the thirst out on the water, Watsons Bay

Acknowledgments

Over the years that this book has been in print, I have received many kind letters from people who have enjoyed it. And the charities that have benefited from the book's royalties are very grateful, so I would like to thank all those readers for their wonderful support.

My thanks to all those people who helped me put this book together in the beginning, especially Dr Don Francois, former Director of Fisheries, New South Wales State Fisheries, the late Mr Mark Joseph, former Chairman of the New South Wales Fish Marketing Authority, Mr Graham Jones, the Authority's former General Manager, and the Sydney Fish Marketing Authority, Pyrmont, which kindly supplied the information on buying and keeping fish. Thank you, George Sautelle, for supplying some of the marvellous pictures of old Watsons Bay.

Thank you, dear Louise Lendrum, who helped me with my typing and battled with my handwriting. I am grateful, too, to all those Australian hosts and hostesses who contributed their favourite recipes.

Thanks also to everyone who helped me with the later editions of this book, including Ben Connolly, Chef and Assistant Manager of our hotel. A very special thank you to my granddaughter, Deborah Irvine, who really read my thoughts. And many thanks, too, to John, our second eldest son, who has helped me so much.

But most of all, thanks to my old Watsons Bay friends, to my late husband, Jack, who ate lots of fish and chips brought home from the restaurant so I could get on with my writing, and to my family, who encouraged me and helped me in this, as they have in so many other things all our lives together.

Index